THE
WAKEFIELD
PONTEFRACT & GOOLE
RAILWAY

BY
C.T. GOODE

Cover picture: An unrecorded WD 2-8-0 leaves Croften Yard with a coal train and heads towards Wakefield past Crofton West Junction. The connection to the GN/GC joint line at Hare Park Jct., goes off to the right. The main line to Pontefract and Goole curves round to the left to Crofton East Junction

A.M. Ross

ISBN 1870313 14 3
72 Woodland Drive, Anlaby, Hull. HU10 7HX

Produced by
Burstwick Print & Publicity Services
Hull.

Contents

Abbreviations.

AJR	Axholme Joint Rlwy.
GNR	Great Northern Rlwy.
H&B	Hull & Barnsley Rlwy.
H&S	Hull & Selby Rlwy.
LNWR	London & North Western Rlwy.
MR	Midland Rlwy.
MS&L	Manchester, Sheffield & Lincolshire Rlwy.
M&LR	Manchester & Leeds Rlwy
NMR	North Midland Rlwy.
NER	North Eastern Rlwy.
WR&GR	West Riding & Grimsby Rlwy.
WP&GR	Wakefield, Pontefract & Goole Rlwy.
Y&NMR	York & North Midland Rlwy
SO, MO, TO etc.	Sats, Mons, Tues only etc.
SX, MX, TX ect.	Sats, Mons, Tues excepted etc.

Foreword

The Lancashire & Yorkshire Railway was formed in 1846 and absorbed a further lot of East Lancashire lines in 1859, leaving it with some 800 locomotives of thirty classes housed in a bevy of small engine sheds which were served by only two railway works. Among these were many tank engines and 86 ex LNWR 0-6-0 tender engines. When Mr. Barton-Wright took over as Loco. Superintendent in 1875 from his time at Swindon, he produced a measure of reasonableness, bringing about standard patterns of 4-4-0 and 0-6-0 types with common boilers, motion and cylinders. On the operating side there was too much in the way of wayside shunting of goods trains and too little protection from the elements at many of the sheds, leading to a great deal of wear and tear. These matters were improved when Mr. Ramsbottom of Crewe became a Director and the Horwich works were founded in 1885, replacing the older ones at Miles Platting and Bury. When Barton-Wright returned to India, J.A.F.Aspinall,also a Crewe man,was appointed in 1886 at the age of 35, and things began to look up. Speeds and efficiency improved on lines crammed with stations and junctions at every corner over a total of 600 miles. Trains were drab, hauled by black engines lined in vermilion and white. Services ran reasonably well and the clientele were undemanding as long as they arrived. To regulate goods traffic control offices were set up in 1912 at Wigan and Wakefield, a forward looking idea.

The line covered here bore all the hallmarks of the L&Y and were a welcome visitor to far-flung parts of the West Riding and never forgotten by the powers that-be at Hunt's Bank, Manchester. Most distinctive were some of the stations and the individualistic signals with their drooping spectacle glasses. The point near Heck where the L & Y, NER and H & B all crossed each other would be the meeting place for some highly contrasting semaphore hardware.

I hope I have covered all the essential and relevant parts of the WP & G history; I am certainly indebted to others who have written before me, and to members of staff at the National Library of Scotland,Leeds,Wakefield,Pontefract and Rotherham libraries for their efforts on my behalf. A word of thanks, too, to Ron Rockett and Peter Cookson for advice and encouragement. The selection of photographs has been better on this occasion.

C. Tony Goode.
Anlaby, Hull.
October 1993

Canals and early Railways

Modes of transport developed as the needs for them became evident) and as commodities which it was desired to move became heavier and greater in bulk, so transport grew in its various forms. The first means were the early, unmetalled roads and the crude carriages which plied on them, also the canals which were a simple and effective developnent of the river, slow yet smooth and efficient.

Canals were relied upon greatly to transfer goods across the Pennines, and there were three of these; first, authorised but not completed until last being the Leeds & Liverpool in 1816, only linked to the Mersey in 1846. Next was the Rochdale canal which ran between the Calder & Hebble at Sowerby Bridge and Manchester, opened in 1804, while the third was the Huddersfield canal, running through Standedge tunnel, built for narrow boats only and linked to Sir John Ramsden's canal which met up with the same Calder & Hebble canal near Cooper Bridge.

Extending eastwards was the Aire & Calder canal and the Knottingley & Goole canal which offered a very important outlet into the Ouse and the Humber. Along the canals industries sprang up, with early coal mines shipping production out of Lancashire on one side of the country to Ireland and abroad,and leaving Yorkshire on the other side through the port of Hull for Europe. Local towns benefitted also through the growth of tile and brickyards and potteries. Around Castleford a vast empire of glassmaking of bottles and jars sprang up. From East Anglia grain came along the coast to the Humber and ran inland along the canals, with coal passing in the opposite direction.

In logical progression the railways came along and were adopted eagerly by any industrialist or entrepreneur with money to invest. Many schemes were mooted, some quite simply silly, but the important ones survived, such as the Manchester & Leeds Railway which took the relatively easy route across the Pennines through Summit tunnel near Rochdale to follow the run of the canal along the Calder valley. The line was the first to cross and almost reached Leeds, arriving in Normanton at Goole Hill Jc. where it joined the North Midland Railway whose lines it had to borrow as far as Leeds Hunslet Road station, thus providing a kind of direct Manchester to Leeds service which had to suffice until the line via Standedge was completed.

The NMR was one of the lines promoted by George Hudson, and ran here from Derby to Leeds. Hudson was a famous York man who, naturally, wished for the best for his own city and, if available, for his own pocket as well. He therefore arranged for the York & North Midland Railway to run from his other Great North of England Railway in York to Gascoigne Wood (near Selby) from 29th. May 1839 and finally south to Altofts Jc. north east of Normanton on the NMR on 30th.June 1840,the

Whitley Bridge station and malthouse, looking west in 1966.

Photo. P. Cookson

appropriate Acts having been passed in Parliament. This new line now gave a clear run between Manchester and York and to all important places beyond, and did much for Normanton's reputation as a junction and refreshment stop. There was also a connection with the Leeds & Selby Railway at Gascoigne Wood, where the line crossed, and eventually a through route to Hull over the Hull & Selby; the potential for industrial growth and passenger traffic was enormous at this time. Hudson was certainly a man to be reckoned with, having a growing network of lines all over the East and North Ridings which were to become a monopoly when they merged into the North Eastern Railway in July 1854.

Early Goole docks

Goole lay at the southern end of this activity and quite long way east of the burgeoning industrial life around Leeds and Wakefield, though linked by its canal which had opened in July 1825, with basins at Goole following one year later. Hudson had thrown his weight behind the idea for a Leeds-Goole railway, which was one of four proposals set before Parliament,

A general view of Goole in the early thirties looking north. The NE station with full yards to the left, while the L & Y line is to the bottom right.

Humberside Libraries

7

namely the Brayton & Goole (Hudson's) off the Leeds & Selby, an idea which would not reach fruition until the first years of the next century, the Goole & Doncaster which anticipated the eventual line from Thorne Jc., something rather vague called the Barnsley & Goole, actually the Manchester, Barnsley & Goole proposed in November 1844 with George Leather & Sons as Engineers who had drawn up a set of plans-this had overtones of the later Hull & Barnsley, and the Wakefield, Pontefract & Goole Railway which sounded practical enough. The latter was favoured as it broke new ground and ran through a coal bearing area. A condition of acceptance was that there should be a branch towards Methley which would give access to Leeds over the NMR. A meeting at Pontefract in 1864 stressed the benefits of such a scheme, as large amounts of corn passed through the markets at Wakefield and there was,of course the outward movement of coal; Pontefract itself was an important agricultural centre,while there were quarries at Knottingley and sandpits at Hensall.

Early Askern and overdue Oakenshaw

Needless to say, George Hudson, in his mantle of NMR and Y & NM interests, was against the proposal, though in fairness it must be said that his methods would have produced a workmanlike job. Instead, the M & L were extremely pleased to become involved with the new line, putting up half the capital towards the estimated cost of £365,000 and placing five directors on the Board. Construction was awarded to a Wakefield man, John Thornton of Kettlethorpe, the Engineer being John Harris. The line was granted its Act on 16th. July 1846, when three additional branches were authorised, namely the desired Pontifract-Methley, one from Knottingley to Askern and a short spur from Oakenshaw to the NMR. The official drawing of the line, itself of great length, shows connections to and from north and south and east and west where the line was to cross the proposed Doncaster to York line near Heck, proving that such plans are often laid well in advance of their execution. On the Askern branch also, a line of just over two miles was intended to run north east from Walden Stubbs across the above York line by a flat crossing near Moss to link up with a proposed Leeds, Wakefield, Pontefract & Grimsby Junction Railway. (The historian's rule would seem to be that the longer the title, the less likely the chance of implementation, as here.) The Askern branch was to be of 10 miles 2 furlongs in total. The length of the main line was to be 26 miles and the crossing with the Doncaster-York line lay at between 17 and 18 miles, with the north spurs each of a little over 3 furlongs and the south spurs at 4 and 5 furlongs. In the event it was left to the Lancashire & Yorkshire company to construct just one of these, the north to east, which actually saw but little use.

At the Goole end the line came south to run parallel with the canal at nearly 25 miles near Rawcliffe Bridge, reaching Goole where it divided into two, the main route running to the Ship Dock in an almost straight line. By the Canal Boat Dock a line ran off north east and round to what was then the Shuffleton Bight, or Murrow Lane Staith, where timber and coal could be received. The projection of the line from Pontefract to Methley ran over the old racecourse in Pontefract Park. This was originally of 1,361 acres, reduced finally to a mere 300, originally available to the Lacy family and their heirs. It was at one time the haunt of all kinds of game used for hunting purposes. The racecourse appeared here on 5th. October 1790, though there had been earlier meetings recorded. Management was in the hands of the Park Trustees, passing in Victorian times to an association of hotel keepers probably at the time when the railway caused it to be moved westwards on the site.

Womersley station   *R. Rockett*

In 1906 the local Corporation took over and it is at present run by a limited company.

At the time of the proposal for the Methley branch the landowners involved locally included the Earl of Mexborough, the Rector of Methley, Mr.Robert Pemberton - Milnes, the Earl of Harewood and, inevitably,the Trustees of the Duchy of Lancaster. On the Askern branch Lord Hawke of Womersley was involved, while nearer Askern the charmingly named Theodosia Brook is recorded.

The Oakenshaw spur was a short one of five furlongs running south from a point near the Barnsley canal and up to the NMR main line at Walton.

Norton station, from an old postcard.   *Colln. P. Cookson*

The opening

The first sod was turned on 24th. September 1846 by Mr. Pemberton-Milnes and on 11th.August 1847 the Directors travelled to Goole on a round of inspection. It was decided as work progressed, largely free of heavy engineering works, that cash payments should be eked out to £17,000 per month and that works on the main line and the Askern branch should not be undertaken with too much haste, so that an opening might be planned for between January and June 1848. This in fact happened on 29th. March 1848 after an inspection had been made by Captain Laffan on the 15th.

The opening days of yore must have been quite bacchantian and certainly very noisy, as the church bells rang in both Wakefield and Goole and at places en route, with a local public holiday declared. At 10.35am a special train of 24 coaches -mere four wheelers, so not as impressive as it sounds-left Wakefield behind two engines, with two bands in open trucks, presumably in the rear away from the smoke. At Pontefract 26 more carriages and an extra engine were added, now making the train somewhat lengthy. Arrival in Goole was at 1.04pm. General traffic commenced on 1st. April 1848. The main festivities seem to have been concentrated on Pontefract, where the residents were perhaps sensitive to the importance which the railway would bring. Of the 700 who rode by the special train, 250 shareholders, directors and others feasted in the Town Hall, while others regaled themselves with a goodly blow-out in 'The Green Dragon'. A contemporary report enthused over the line, referring several times to its bridges, the 'pretty one' of two arches over the rise of the spur line to the NMR, which it also crossed, the engineering feat of burrowing beneath the NMR main line at Oakenshaw without unduly disturbing that company's traffic.

Interior of Wakefield Kirkgate station, with station box.   *M.A. King*

At Sharlston was an overbridge provided for Lord Westmoreland and tenants leading to one the estate lodges, of handsome Swiss cottage style and the possible explanation for the similar station buildings found here and there on the main line and Askern branch. Perhaps the architect was impressed? At Featherstone a brick overbridge was provided for the Prince of Wales (in theory) as Duke of Lancaster, while at Knottingley came a span of 80ft. over the canal.

As we have been name-dropping, it is permissible to continue and mention other landowners adjacent to the line and not unsympathetic to it; Lord Beaumont at Carlton Hall, Viscount Downe of Cowick Hall, Snaith and Ralph Creyke, Magistrate, of Rawcliffe Hall.

The Swiss cottage station buildings appeared at various places such as Knottingley originally and at Womersley, and were described as being of 'white brick'. Approaching Goole could be seen a 'new and beautiful Gothic church with a handsome spire, forming a conspicuous and pleasing object as you approach the town'. At the time of the line's opening the church had not been consecrated and was not ready for services; the Aire & Calder Canal Company had to surrender the land on which it stood, for franchise. A short Act of Parliament was thus needed before God could be praised for His bounty. The terminal station was next to the church, in the 'York' style and with a roof of 100 ft. overall, partly covering two platforms of 220 ft. length and with two centre lines:-

At the opening the dock provision in Goole was as follows

Railway	600 x 250 ft.	Packet	490 x 360 ft.
Outer	250 x 200 ft.	Barge	900 x 150 ft.
	Ship 600 x 310 ft.		

with a connection between two of them of 200 x 70 ft. The total dock area was about 16 acres.

The Askern branch opened speedily on 6th. June 1848, but the Oakenshaw spur was held up from August 1848 and so little was done that the line did not open until July 1861. Here was a cheap tender of £7,900. Work was stopped until 10th. August 1859 after a fresh tender had been offered by a different builder, for £6,360. He undertook to remove the shoddy parts and start again. The L & Y ran a passenger service from Wakefield to Oakenshaw, reversing at the junction with the MR to reach the station, this until 1st. June 1870 when the station was closed and replaced by Sandal & Walton to the south. The service lasted until 1887

No. 56 002 on a mgr train at Ackton Hall, August 1985.　　　　*S. Batty*

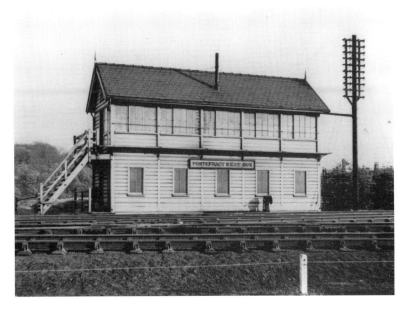

Above:Pontefract West signal box

Pontefract Libraries

Below: The contrasting East box.

The GN & Methley

One good reason why the Askern branch and that from Pontefract to Methley were completed so expeditiously was that they furthered the ambitions of the Great Northern Railway who were promoting a route from London to the North via York and had obtained powers to run trains from an end-on junction with the WP & G at a point 2 miles 39 chains beyond Askern from 1st. May 1847, along the short branch from Doncaster through Stocksbridge, later Arksey. From Knottingley GN trains then ran to Monkhill and over the other branch to Methley Jc., from where the NMR had granted running powers to Leeds on 16th. October 1847. There were five daily L & Y trains each way from Wakefield to Stocksbridge, and two on Sundays. Thus the WP & G was exercising its own tit for tat running powers.

In 1847 a short line of three miles was promoted from Burton Salmon, north of Knottingley, round eastwards into the latter town's station to enable Y & NM trains to run to Doncaster over the Askern branch. This agreement was formalised on 29th. November 1850, in which year the GN began to run its passenger services. Some of these went to Wakefield

144006 on 1622 Goole to Leeds at Rawcliffe. July 1987   *S. Batty*

Kirkgate which became their terminus, a puny affair of 'a small wooden hut with a platform in front' in 1851. What little it possessed was, nevertheless, owned jointly with the L & Y from August 1853, with a rebuilding in 1857,though its use as a terminus by the GN ceased at that time, when that company's trains chuffed up the spur to a new station at Westgate. On the opening of the West Riding & Grimsby line from Doncaster to Leeds in 1866, GN activity over the L & Y was heavily reduced. Knottingley was also jointly owned with the GN, and the contractor, George Thomson, rebuilt the station in 1854 with four platforms and an overall roof, an easier job than at Kirkgate where the raised formation had to be widened to take an island platform and the weight of an overall roof.

In 1871 the through line from Doncaster to York via Selby was opened by the NER and the earlier proposed spur from north-east near Hensall was put in. This seems to have been little used, however, though it would have afforded a shorter route between Goole and York and a route to York for H & B services if running powers could have been wrung out of the NER! It closed about 1905.

The L & Y, as expected, objected to the direct line to York, seeing that it would remove the lucrative GN traffic from its own lines, It was somewhat mollified, however, to receive running powers into York and sanction for the above mentioned spur at Hensall. On completion of the branch from Selby to Goole by the NER, the latter was no longer needed in any case.

'Heritage' dmu at Knottingley on Goole to Leeds service. March 1984

Another, rather remarkable fact was that the original 1845 Act made provision for a line from Crofton running north west to the NMR line just north of Oakenshaw station. This was never implemented, however, until the LMS Act of 1927 enabled the line to be opened a year later.

The MR looked after the collieries alongside its own lines and had its own branches from Snydale Jc., north of Oakenshaw, to the intriguingly named Don Pedro and Featherstone Main, which latter was approached from its north side, as opposed to the L & Y which served the opposite flank. These branches were opened in 1885; the MR was refused passenger train services on the branches, probably for miners' excursions, in 1897.

Stations on the Goole branch were not a complete set on the opening of the line, with Crofton opening on 1st. November 1853, Sharlston in 1869 and Tanshelf appearing in September 1871. This station had 'Pontefract' added to its name on 1st. December 1936. All survived ultimately, except Crofton which went on 30th.November 1931, leaving Hare Park & Crofton on the nearby WR & G to cope for a further 21 years. Sharlston lasted until 3rd. March 1958.

The branch from Pontefract Monkhill to Methley Jc. was really a corridor for the transit of GN service initially, with a passenger service supplied by that company from 1st. October 1849. There was one station on the line, at Castleford Cutsyke, which did not open until 1860 and was somewhat of a token halt from the look of its poor buildings and distance from the town.

Staking claims

Seeing the GN rather perkily exercising its running powers into far flung parts,the L & Y, mindful of the fact that it had no outlet for its colliery traffic directly to London, and certainly no passenger terminus in the capital, laid plans on 23rd.September 1864 for an ambitious railway of 113 miles to run from Askern through Lincoln and Peterborough along an earlier route plotted by the GN to Long Stanton near Cambridge, all this with the agreement of the GER who would permit access to Liverpool Street station. Some doubts were cast over the estimates tendered and of course the GN objected vigorously; the Bill was defeated on a second reading by 41 votes on 14th.March 1865.The Act also included a 13 mile branch from Haxey (Lincs) to Goole which would broadly link the ends of the Askern and Goole branches and serve a flat and soggy wasteland, fit only for cutting peat. Later on, however, the L & Y was to combine with the NER ownership of the Axholme Joint Railway which had its 'main' line from just south of Goole to Haxey Jc. on the GN & GE Joint line, the company being physically detached from its other line at Goole.

Nos. 31 156 and 31 280 pass Knottingley West Jc. on a sand train in July 1986
S. Batty

It would seem, then, that the Askern branch was not merely built by the L & Y to accommodate GN interests, but formed part of a useful expansion potential, firstly for coal, then for passenger development far and wide. The reader will remember, also, the branch projected to a nebulous Wakefield, Pontefract & Grimsby Junction scheme which never materialised but almost certainly would track across eastwards through that same soggy waste land through Reedness Jc. found later on the AJR, along the line of the future Fockerby branch, across the Trent and then joining up the ends of sundry branches at Winterton and Barton-on-Humber, with a vast and giddy prospect of the Humber estuary with its opportunites for exporting beautiful coal. The MS&L was a line with which the L & Y had not particularly worked, except at Huddersfield and Barnsley, while the growing monopoly of the NER certainly called for something independent, so why not stake a claim on the Lincs. side of the river, however, such dreams were not to be fulfilled.

17

WD No. 90615 looms with an eastbound coal train at Tanshelf in December 1963   *R. Rockett*

Claim-staking was not successful in the direction of Immingham and the L & Y obtained only the rather flimsy AJR towards the end of its separate existence, a little line whose life revolved mainly round peat and sugar beet. Even at this late stage the L & Y tried its hardest, with ideas for a five mile long line from Epworth on the AJR to Hatfield, opened in 1909 and a further 8$\frac{1}{2}$ mile Hatfield Moor Further Extension Railway to Black Carr Jc. to the south east of Doncaster, where its own Dearne Valley Railway came in from Wakefield. Fortunately, perhaps,the Extension was not built, as the terrain was neither promising nor hospitable.

The AJR was finally built on a line of route projected by George Hudson, that section from Haxey to Crowle which was to be part of the long link between his Eastern Counties Railway and the Y & NMR, an idea which was wound up in 1854. The GN, too, had tried for a line from Gainsborough through Crowle to the Askern branch, but without success. The NER soon saw off the opposition and bought the two most important railways on the Isle of Axholme. The L & Y joined with the NER in promoting these lines, hoping to reach the new collieries of South Yorkshire over yet a further new branch,from Haxey to Tickhill near

Doncaster, where the action lay for a time. However, powers for this line were transferred to the GN in 1898 and a sketchy line materialised as far as Bawtry only, leaving the L & Y as partner in a virtual non-starter. With distant Goole to be reached via Haxey, there is little wonder that nothing significant developed.

Goole - Gilberdyke schemes

What else was new, then except to try to reach Hull on the north bank of the Humber,where the NER was already establishing quite a monopoly over the fish, timber and general traffic. There was a tantalising gap in the railway map between Goole and the point where the old Hull & Selby line came closest at Gilberdyke, caused by the crossing required of the Ouse at Hook. However, several companies were formed who were willing to take on the expense, as the Hull & West Riding Junction Railway, also the Hull, Goole and Doncaster Railway which was registered in May 1855, both of which presaging the Hull & Barnsey which was to appear thirty years later and proved to be the success which these two were certainly not. The line of route followed that of the H & B to North Cave,then turned south to Gilberdyke and Goole where it was to ioin the L & Y and meet the SYR at Thorne. A connection would also have been made at South Cave with the line to York at Market Weighton. The failure here was due to lack of finance and an idea which was perhaps ahead of its time.

Strong Trio at Kirkgate; Nos. 31 563, 110 and 549.   *S. Batty*

The evening pick-up goods leaves Monkhill for Wakefield c. 1955, headed by No. 52186   *P. Cookson*

A second venture was one by the South Yorkshire Railway, northwards from its line at Thorne, supported by the GN and which would run to Gilberdyke, eventually called Staddlethorpe. Thirdly came the Doncaster, Goole & Hull Railway, an L & Y plan with which we are more directly concerned and which led L & Y traffic off the WP & G to the same point at Staddlethorpe, for Hull.

In the event it was the covetous NER who won the day with its own plans for a line from the same Staddlethorpe to Goole and Thorne; the company had, of course, objected furiously to everyone else's schemes. This one passed through the Commons but was defeated in the Lords by just one vote. In time the Act was presented again and passed on 27th. July 1863, the line opening on 2nd. August 1869. The SYR was allowed to run some coal traffic between Thorne and Hull in exchange for NER running powers to Doncaster. As far as the L & Y was concerned its traffic could be brought to Hull at the same rates via Goole as by way of Normanton and Selby, using new running powers swapped with the NER enabling it to reach Normanton and Barnsley. The L & Y did not actually use its running powers to Hull until 1880; it had had interests prior to that year, however, in the shape of direotors on the Board of the Hull Dock Company.

The Doncaster, Goole & Hull Junction was a proposal of November 1862 which comprised four Railways. No.1 was the main route from Thorne Jc. to Goole and on to Staddlethorpe. No. 2 was a spur from the WP & G at Airmin Pasture (sic) to No. 1 just short of the crossing gates at Goole, while Railway No. 3 was a short spur off, just south of this eastwards to what was then known as the Bight branch which ran to the Ouse. Beyond the crossing of the river at Skelton occurred the most interesting proposal, for Railway No. 4 would leave No. 1 to run north for almost three miles to reach Howden, where a terminal station would be situated at the corner of Hallgate and Wesley Place. Had this little line come into being, it would have given much life to Howden which would have been linked to its bigger neighbour and useful main routes into the West Riding and the south. However, it was not to be and Howden suffered two stations, one too far distant to be of real use, the other pretentious and well-placed but on a line which offered little to passengers.

The line described: Wakefield to Crofton

Faced with a map of the south side of Wakefield, one is somewhat overawed by the impression which the L & Y railway lines have made upon it, forming as they did, and still do to some extent, a large triangular layout on the slopes down to the Calder which executes a bend beneath Wakefield road bridge, shortened by the canal cut across it. The later WR & G line came up from the south well to the left of the scene to enter Westgate station, while its own sidings and the like were out to the north at Wrenthorpe.

The course of the old L & Y main line comes in from the south west, beneath the arches of the WR & G, sporting only two tracks in 1914 before a further two were added. South of the line were corn mills (Mark Lane and West Riding), with sidings connecting them, before the lines fanned out into four to enter Kirkgate station and the GN spur came down the slope from Westgate to the north, to reach the lines at Ings Road Jc. The skeleton of the system still exists. The station had an overall roof covering the side platform on the north side and the main island, whose outer face afforded a view of the Calder Vale industrial estate with a steel boat and boiler works, two engineering premises (Rose and Phoenix), the canal boatyard, a glassworks and ammonia works, all very entertaining when waiting for a train if they were in full swing and the prevailing wind was a strong one! The station premises were in a hotch-potch of a long building on the north side, partly two-storeyed and overlooking an equally depressing workaday part of the city, with a walk down Park street to

No. 56 092 brings an empty mgr working round the curve to Crofton West Jc. in August 1985   *S. Batty*

catch a tram into the centre of things. The platforms were linked by a rather dismal subway, one of those with long ramps at each side which seem to take ages to surmount. Very recently, after many years of neglect, this particular one has been livened up by a coat of light paint. Accompanying the station buildings on the north side was a large goods depot and a set of sidings which were extended eastwards for some distance along the side of the main line towards Normanton, overlooked by the Union Workhouse. To the south of this line, within the triangle of running lines were the sorting sidings and carriage shed of nine through roads. Up and Down lines ran behind the station on the south side, as indeed today, and ran round to the south to form the west flank of the triangle, receiving connections from the station and from the main line at the east end. On the east side of this curve were the twelve roads of Whitham's Sidings, which came together to the south at the signal box on the down side, and a general goods yard and warehouse on the west side connected by a roadway from Kirkgate south of the underbridge which also served the Calder Vale estate. Kirkgate East signal box was just outside the station, within the fork and had 153 levers, of which 121 were in use. The east-south side of this vast triangle came out of things quite simply, apart from three extra through lines on the west side, and all resolved itself in due course into the junction at the southern tip which was

Above: The rather bashful Swiss cottage station building at Featherstone.
L & Y Society

Below: Plenty of room for the signalmen at Wakefield East.   M.A. King

delayed a little as four lines running parallel for a short diatance before becoming two to cross the river at Calder Bridge Jc. From here a couple of extra running lines ran on the west side towards the station and goods yard entrance.

The junction signal box lay across the river to the south, and after this temporary bottleneck sidings appeared once more on the down side marking the locomotive depot and turntable, this being as a result some way out of town and often causing halts by local train services to give lifts for enginemen to and from the station, There were running loops on both sides of the line here, as far as Oakenshaw Jc., and the shed outlet decanted out over its own spur across the Aire & Calder canal to reach the main running lines. At Oakenshaw Jc. the short spur up to the MR main line at Sandal & Walton left on the south side, with the signal box on the same side. Across the two sets of lines is the 'pretty bridge', one arch for each and joining two fields. The road from Agbrigg to Walton contrives to span one line and dive beneath the other alongside the MR main line which crossed before the next set of junctions was reached at Crofton, first West Jc. which sent off the long spur to the WR & G at Hare Park, an important one, this, for GN traffic requiring Kirgate station; by this route it was possible for trains to serve Westgate as well. First this junction, then signal box on the south side, and then straight on for the Dearne Valley line to the Doncaster area with its own neat sidings on the south side of what became another triangular junction, with Crofton South Jc. at one extremity and East Jc. at the other. Our line ran round to the north east to East Jc., with an extra loop on the south side and signal box beyond the junction on the north side. The north-east side of the triangle had a couple of through sidings on the outer side. Beyond Crofton East Jc. in 1914 was an up loop, and after 1923 in LMS days a sinuous spur was put in to join the MR line at Oakenshaw, this running from north to west. The connection was originally planned by the WP & G but not carried out, Between the lines the main A638 road manages to wend its way over the MR and beneath the L & Y en route to Sharlston. Close to this point came Crofton station at 2¹/₂ miles, with a minor road crossing to the west of it and no habitation, in fact Crofton and New Crofton lay at some distance to the south, the nearest being a straggle of houses on the main road. Crofton was served by the WR & G station close by, and the L & Y premises were seen off, with attendant signal box, in 1931.

The line has been climbing steadily, with the steepest gradient at 1 in 131 to come before Sharlston station waa reached at 4 miles, a relatively rural run in cutting for the most part before the mining 'corridor', which was one of the reasons for the line's existence, was reached. At Sharlston signal box south of the line a neat triangular single line junction was to be found on the opposite side, leading to eight through sidings and to Sharlston colliery, after which the branch ran to the Midland line nearby at Snydale Sidings. On the down side was a long refuge siding for 56

Calder Bridge Jc., looking south.   *M.A. King*

wagons, with the up platform of Sharlston station adjacent to the signal box. The down was over the level crossing (Gin Lane) and had the station buildings. North of these was the village, not Sharlston, as might have been expected, but Streethouse, which the railway company seemed to have overlooked. This was rectified recently when a new halt was opened further east at Whinny Lane level crossing. In the matter of nomenclature the L & Y could be as perverse as the NER, There were in fact three Sharlstons, New Sharlston a mile away at the colliery, Sharlston Common, equidistant but south of the line, and the largest, with Sharlston which was probably the original and further away still, linked to the station and colliery across the fields by footpath. The first purpose built mining village in the West Riding was founded here, and large scale mining commenced at New Sharlston colliery in 1865.

In June 1993 the press reported the closure of this, Yorkshire's oldest pit, after 28 years of production, putting almost 400 miners out of work. The colliery had not been due to close until the following September, but the date was brought forward.

Sharlston to Featherstone

From here the line entered real colliery country, with the general gradient falling, to rise again through Featherstone. The run to this village was dominated by Victoria Colliery which occupied the south side of the line, with Streethouse West signal box on the south side covering the level crossing and an up refuge siding for 34 wagons, before the line took on loops on both sides between Snydale West and east on north and south sides of the line respectively. The colliery here had a neat site and layout which extended between the railway and the Pontefract road to the south of it, the site being closed off to the east by the B 6133 road overbridge. Old Snydale village and the Hall lay along this road the north. One small query would be to enquire why, if there was a Streethouse west signal box, there was not an east. There does not seem to have been much room to accommodate one, apart from a minor road crossing. The Author has, however, seen a small reference to such a cabin during a perusal of working notices. Opposite here was one of the original coal pits sunk prior to the laying of the railway line, on its south side and in the vicinity of Pontifract Barracks-early fatigues perhaps?

Beyond the road overbridge just mentioned came a fresh set of sidings on the north side, nine dead end and four through alongside a down loop line, before the sidings signal box was reached to the north, next to another single line triangle of lines, this one not so obvious among the pointwork and forming the start of a long mineral branch to the colliery about half a mile to the north. Samuel Cunliffe Lister of Manningham Mills

Sharlston station looking west, with rather bleak vistas and a humdrum building.   *L & Y Society*

in Bradford purchased what was then the small colliery at Featherstone and made it into one of the best mines in the area by 1870. The small village of Featherstone soon grew in size to reach a population of 20,000. Ridiculoualy close to the sidings signal box was Featherstone Colliery cabin on the south side at the east end of the triangle, controlling the down loop and yard exit of Ackton Hall Colliery across the lines, which was hard by, with all the processing and headgear to the north, and spoil heap to the south, both connected by a private line crossing by an overbridge. The MR branch line from Snydale had also arrived from the north, with its own attendant sidings, even managing to serve a brick works on the way.

Featherstone sprawled some distance each side of the B6421 road north and south, with the level crossing, of the railway and the station to the west of it, in the centre of the village, There were parallel platforms with the main buildings on the south side, a little unexpectedly of full blown Swiss cottage type, looking rather like a dowager in a dustbin. The station signal box, a large wooden one, was prominent at the south side of the level crossing and to the east of it. Beneath the shadow of the spoil heap lay the Hippodrome and Palace theatres, the latter next to the signal box, while to the south was the model development of Featherstone Square with the public bathhouse as its centrepiece. A short way further along the Wakefield road lay the charminly named village of Purston Jaglin, more reminiscent of a hero in a Wodehouse novel.

Featherstone signal box, with station building beyond.   *M.A. King*

The line enjoyed a respite from its surroundings now, being straight and in deep cutting for the run, first up at 1 in 132, then down the long 1 in 150 for three miles to Knottingley, which must have given a fillip to many a heavy coal train. At the end of the cutting and in Pontefract Park came Tanshelf station, nemed after that particular portion of Pontefract and a late-comer, which is surprising in view of the proximity to the race course, not appearing until September 1873. Tanshelf was at the edge of the business part of the town with two markets down Front street and a considerable local population. The railway neatly marked the boundary between this densely built up area and the parkland to the north, which the main road entered by an overbridge. The station lay to the north of this with its rather dull buildings of single storey on the town side complete with a heavy glass awning. Here, too, was a small goods yard on the town side, of three roads with the signal box overlooking the slip points on the north side. In best L & Y tradition there were extras in the shape of two refuge lines on the up side east of the road bridge. The new Tanshelf station, opened in May 1992 now stands on the site of these sidings, very smart with long ramps down to the platforms. One noticeable feature in the distance on the town approach is the big Victorian edifice known as the Queen's Hotel, one time Victoria, having the features of a railway hotel and near enough to the line to be considered as such. There would be rollicking days when punters passed on the way to have a flutter, or returned to console themselves over their losses.

Assorted structures at Featherstone on a cut-back platform   *M.A. King*

Wakefield and Pontefract as towns

Having reached Pontefract we can now pause and reflect a little on the merits or otherwise of the places served by the railway in question, leaving Goole until journey's end is reached in due course. Wakefield, in 1901, had a population of 42,000 rising to 75,838 today,and three market days. The city has little that is 'touristy' and, to quote the writer at the turn of the century, 'while at one time the centre of the Yorkshire cloth trade, it has subsided into a half bucolic, half manufacturing position, with a dash of the old days about it but little quaintness, 'Possibly these observations are vague, to say the least, especially the use of 'bucolic', but the author did go on to say that the city had a good skyline, which is true today, The parish church of All Saints dominates this, with its highly crocketed spire of 247 ft., the tallest in Yorkshire and standing in the best position in town. It became a cathedral in fairly recent times, 1888, and underwent restoration by Giles Gilbert Scott, with the organ enlarged in 1879 and extensions eastwards in 1901. Adjacent is one of the earlier and still one of the best indoor shopping precincts, which is popular over a wide area. Other large structures of note are the classical Corn Exchange and modern Town Hall. At the road bridge over the Calder mentioned earlier is a chantry chapel, built for road - side prayer. This particular one was built in the reign of Edward III, then rebuilt by Edward IV in memory of those who fell at the battle of Wakefield in 1460 what exists today owes much to alterations made around 1850.

Not strictly on route, but in January 1960 the first train to Leeds Cen., waits to leave Pontefract Baghill.   P. Cookson

Pontefract is a smaller place, with 13,500 in 1901 and 29,047 today, but more interesting and noted historically. The castle ruins are not far from the railway, on a rock and at one time covering seven acres, with seven round towers and curtain walls. Portions of the Keep and Dungeons survive; one is 25 ft. deep with an entry only at the top. Originally the castle was founded by Ilbert de Lacy, then passed to the Earl of Lancaster in the 14th. century. He had the doubtful privilege of being beheaded, in his own castle here, after defeat at the battle of Boroughbridge. In 1400 Richard II was brought to Pontefract for imprisonment where, according to various reports, he was either beheaded, starved to death or escaped to Scotland; one takes one's pick. Several other crowned heads have visited the castle, and one thing is certain, they did not arrive by train! The churches catch the eye in Pontefract. All Saints nearby was ruined during the Civil Wars and was repaired in 1834, with interesting results. St.Giles in the town has an octagonal upper tower with an open crown.

At some time the grounds of the castle were used as a field for the growing of liquorice which was cultived for making 'Pomfret cakes',those black,floppy discs embossed with a picture of the castle and made from the thickened juice of the plant root. Once whole fields of the plant were cultivated here, including the area on which the castle ruins stand.

Tanshelf station from the approach. *Pontefract Libraries*

The rather splendid main building of Monkhill.   *Pontefract Libraries*

Pontefract had, and still has, three stations, having regained Tanshelf last year; it bacame known as Pontefract Tanshelf on lst. December 1936. This station is possibly the easiest to reach, being on a straight run out of town. Monkhill (8½m.) is ¾ miles further on and has the advantage of being also on the route of trains on the Methley branch, though it is not so far from the town. However, there is a long dip in the approach road and a stiff pull up the hill into the main shopping area which is deterring. Baghill, on the Swinton & Knottingley Joint line, is the longest and most convenient, though situated low and giving pedestrians another sharp rise into the town centre. Bag hill behind the station runs close to the 200 ft. contour, while the castle itself is a mere 142 ft.

Chalk and cheese might be the phrase to define the difference between Monkhill and Tanshelf stations, the former having obviously been designed and built with a great deal of care, comprising a two storey building set centrally and flanked on each side by a single storey gable, each linked by a recessed area in which were the offices and entrances. Though obviously needing barge boards, the building was given a pleasing and somewhat Tudor appearance by quoins at the corners of the building. Tanshelf was the opposite in character, coming later to the scene, obviously at a time of financial economy. The building as it faced the road was a take-it-or-leave-it single storey oblong box with three windows, a single doorway and no embellishment, though looking a little more businesslike when one stepped beneath the deep canopy on to the platform.

31

Pontefract to Knottingley

At Pontefract East Jc. the spur line opened on 19th. May 1879 concurrently with the S & K Joint line ran round south to reach the S & K station at Baghill, where regular service of trains from Leeds via Castleford could run neatly to its own terminal bays independently of the main through lines. The A645 was crossed by a high arched viaduct which still survives at the time of writing, topped with various growths of young saplings and the like.

Beyond Pontefract the line enters a very active transport area in a shallow gap where the river Aire turns to flow north-south for a short distance at Brotherton and Ferrybridge, with the river and a canalised part of it, the A1 main road and A162 which begins its run to York, a minor road and a necklace of power lines from Ferrybridge power station all jostling for position to pass through. Then, of course, there is the railway line to York which threw off sidings to the power station and owned a station at Ferrybridge, closed on 13th. September 1965. From here the S & K began its run south through Baghill, and south of Ferrybridge the original line ran round north-east to the Goole line at Knottingley, opened chiefly to accommodate the GN through services to and from York. Powers for this 2½ mile link from Burton Salmon, built by the Y & NM, were obtained on 9th. July 1847 and trains were able to use the facility from 8th. August 1850.

Knottingley 'A' Jc. (in distance) with train heading west   *C.T. Goode*

A WD and brake van try out the new loop at Monkhill East Goods Jc. in 1966. The line is now single.   *P. Cookson*

In 1903, from a point where the S & K set off, the L & Y proposed to put in a long north-west spur to the WP & G line as part of improvements at Monkhill station, as the company was having difficulties in running its Liverpool/Manchester to York/Newcastle expresses over the MR lines at Normanton and wished instead to route them via Pontefract and then to the NER at Ferrybridge. There would be a new station some 100 yd. to the west at Monkhill, which would have been more convenient for the town but which, like Tanshelf, would have been beyond the Methley line junction, and there would have been a loop for non-stopping trains, plus new sidings, bays and island platforms. The shed at Knottingley would have been transferred here and workings would have been extended here from Knottingley. Such was not to be, however, and it was not until 26th. July 1965 that the spur was in fact opened, primarily for coal traffic to the power station and making a three way junction, across the base of which the line under review passes on its way to Knottingley (10$\frac{1}{2}$m.). Today the site is closed off by the M62 which run east-west while the A1 has been improved with good intersections and a service area.

Before Knottigley station is reached (10$\frac{1}{2}$ miles) the spur from Ferrybridge comes in from the north at the 'A' signal box, set on the south side with 44 levers, which with 'B' at the east end attended to the station working here. Obviously the powers that be were a little short of ideas for names for the signal cabins here, a curious waste of opportunity which the

NER would certainly have made good use of, with its liking for the grand and impressive in nomenclature. There were four platforms at Knottingley, the side one with main buildings, No.1, then an island with faces Nos.2 and 3 and a completing side platform No.4. This originally faced outwards to its running line, the down from Aakern, while the inner side of the island was at some time named Middle Siding. Later evidence shows differently, however, with the outer platform facing the correct way. There were a pair of parallel overall roofs of triangular end section, somewhat dismal to stand beneath, with a footbridge linking the platforms at the west end. The single storey station buildings, goods shed and coal yard were all on the north side and the station was in fact some distance from the town which lay to the east near the Aire and north of the line. 'B' cabin, also of 44 levers, lay in the fork of the main line and branch to Askern which struck off southwards here. South of the station were extensive sidings and the small engine shed of just a single road, closed in July 1922, and its turntable, the access to all this being controlled from 'A' box. Curiously, access to and from Headlands Glass works siding was over the turntable. The walk into the town was a pleasant road, past the Hall and with the brewery on the north side set back in a sylvan setting. Once over the canal one had arrived, though apart from St.Botolph's church and the White Swan there was little to hold the visitor.

Perhaps better, then, to return to the railway and traverse the line eastwards with slow lines on each side past Knottingley Depot West, 36 levers on the north side, where the spur, opened to goods on 29th. March 1915 came round from the Askern branch, then across England Lane to Knottingley Sidings, a coal depot and goods yard on the south side, and the Depot East signal box with its level crossing and outlet to the extensive premises of the Glass Bottle Works on the north side. These works also had facilities alongside the canal. South of the line is a considerable residential part of Knottingley in two areas, one close to the newer curve, the other east and near the sand quarries.

An excursion working runs west from Tanshelf, headed by a 'Black Five' locomotive.   *P. Cookson*

Whitley Bridge to Hensall

Once Knottingley is left behind, the line becomes more rural in character and certainly flatter, with a curve first to the north east and then east to cross the canal, reaching Kellingley colliery, opened 1965 on the north side. There was originally a Kellingley gate box, taking the name from a hamlet close by. Next came Sudforth Lane crossing with the signal box north of the line, once innocuous, then becoming large and modern looking to mark the entrance to the new colliery nearby. More important, perhaps, was that by 1907 a stretch of four tracks had been laid here, with slow lines put in on each side as far as Whitley Bridge, the next station ($14^3/_4$ m.). Here stragglers could be laid aside while the fast expresses ran through, utilising the water troughs which were placed here to replenish supplies and, one might suspect, save money on water charges if this commodity were to be taken on NER territory. There were also water cranes adjacent to the slow lines for goods trains here, and the whole system was heated in winter. This was one of ten such on the L & YR. There were also cranes at the east and west ends of Whitley Bridge station for good measure. The next troughs going west were at Horbury Jc. on the main line, then at Smithy Bridge nearer to Manchester. Water was also available at Knottingley on the down side (Goole platform) and in both directions on the Askern platforms.

Whitley Bridge station, a pleasant building.   *L & Y Society*

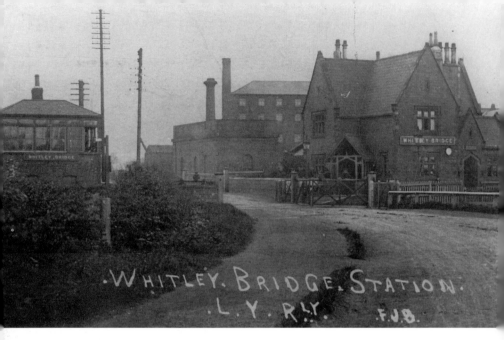

An early postcard of Whitley Bridge looking rather seedy.   *C.T. Goode*

In 1912 one of those wordy instructions appeared in the Working Appendix:

'When the engine of an up goods train fails to take water when passing over the troughs at Whitley Bridge, the train must be brought to a stand at Sudforth Lane signal box and the signalman informed of the fact by the driver in order that arrangements may be made with Knottingley for the train to proceed thereto or for it to be shunted into one of the two loop lines at Sudforth Lane whilst the engine returns to Whitley Bridge to replenish its water supply there.'

There were a couple of sidings to the south of the running lines adjacent to the slow road, presumably for the above purpose and to hold traffic at busy times. It is interesting that part of the old up goods line still exists at the present time and is used for storing spare coal wagons.

At Whitley Bridge the turnouts into four lines took place to the west of the level crossing here, and in a slightly unusual manner in that the two new lines were added to the north side and the lines then redesignated slow-fast-fast-slow. The smallish goods yard lay on the south side, with the station building of decidedly gaunt appearance adjacent to the level crossing, The parallel platforms lay across the roadway to the east, with the signal box on the west side. The cabin was of the Smith & Yardley type which looked its age (1875), and yet was said to be pleasant to work in. Beyond the station to the east, a siding served a corn mill and artificial manure factory, known as the Patent National Fertilisation Syndicate, to the north.

Hensall Jc. signal box with staff.

P. Cookson

Hensall station, looking west in 1959.

Whitley Bridge itself was over the canal which was close by the railway at this point, while the village of Whitley lay strung out along the A19 some way beyond. In recent years the canal bridge proved rather weak, so that passengers on the double deck buses had to alight and walk over while their vehicle crossed empty. To the north and much closer was the hamlet of Eggborough, though latterly rather impeded by the M62 motorway. Here too was Eggborough power station, and from Whitley Bridge a layout was put in for merrygoround coal trains, this having at first access from both directions.

On the straight running east at 16½m. was Hensall station, the line first crossing the A645 at a gate box which must have seen much activity, especially at summer weekends. Hensall station had its own crossing for the road which led to the village just to the north, small and complete, except for its church, St. Paul's which stands aloof back beyond the station on the main road, offering villagers a good walk to receive those two great Motivators in life, railways and religion. Somewhere in high places it was decided to preserve as much of Hensall station as possible, as obviously happened at Hebden Bridge; here are still the Swiss cottage main building on the north side of the line, the wooden shelter on the south and the Smith & Yardley box in use, disguising quite well the control panel within, but rather hidden by a colour light signal outside. Things are helped along in that an obvious steam enthusiast occupies the house, if the advertising signs and a traction engine in the yard are anything to go by. West of the level crossing on the south was a siding to malt houses, while a small goods yard of two lines was at the opposite end, north side, the outlet extended for a short way to take in the siding from the sand quarry here. The Hensall Sand Quarry had a few of its very own red wagons for deliveries to customers. Still further beyond was the Heck Ings gatehouse supervising the road out of the village at this end.

Snaith to Rawcliffe

From here to the next station at Snaith was one of the most interesting sections of the WP & G line, for at the point where the main line to York was crossed there were to be connecting spurs for each direction which would, in effect have created three way junctions on both lines at four points of the compass. In the event, only the north-east spur was built and it is difficult to fathom what extra traffic might have been generated by constructing the other three; as it was, the spur which did appear, on lst. April 1848, had lost its usefulneas by the year 1905. However, things became lively enough hereabouts when the H & B came across both existing railways from the north east to south west in 1885, planning a station at Heck which also never materialised, but sending a more useful spur down westwards to the L & Y line at Hensall Jc. Add in an aerodrome here and a Borstall institution, plus the station at Heck on the NER line, and life here was complete for a time.

Hensall Jc. was a 'proper' L & Y cabin on the south side of the junction, with 36 levers of which eight were spare, linked with Gowdall Jc. at the H & B end of the spur. That company had a two road engine shed here on the uphill side of the spur and three sidings off the downhill side, the L & Y with four sidings on the flat on the north side of the line. By a facing point it was possible for H & B trains to run directly to these sidings or to draw ahead and back into their own yard without fouling the L & Y line. On the H & B layout was a 49 ft. turntable, and the shed seems to have been a resting place for engines and crews between duties.

Hensall Jc's signalman had the task of reporting to Goole the times at which Hull-bound trains passed his cabin, also to advise Goole and Methley Jc. of details of empty wagons which were in transit. The spur up to the H & B line and the latter's old route through as far as Drax power station remains open for merrygoround workings; the traffic thereover rattles through the old Carlton Towers station much brisker than anything which ever passed before. The junction is controlled from Hensall station, while the old main line to Goole becomes single here.

The line was now truly rural, passing firstly beneath the H & B main line and, a little way further on the H & B and GC joint line, which was an unsuccessful latecomer of 1916 which passed here through the village of Gowdall. On the WP & G there was no station at Gowdall, though there were a couple of isolated sidings which could hold up to eighty wagons on the up side, available for both directions and worked from a ground frame.

Snaith, another glorious building.   *L & Y Society*

The WP & G line next turned a little to the northeast to enter Snaith station (20$\frac{1}{4}$ m.), where a big village is set south of the line between it and the main road and, in the centre, a road also strikes north to Selby across the Aire through Carlton, where one of the seats of the Duke of Norfolk is situated about two miles from the station. The buildings here were quite substantial though rather plain looking, of red brick with three gables along the front and two at the ends, a fact which was thought interesting enough to attract the local gentry and which caused the halting of the best train of the day for many years. The structure was on the village side of the line next to parallel platforms. West of the level crossing with the Selby road was a ridiculous, short siding on the south side, later extended to serve the premises of the Snaith Clog Sole company, which really did describe what was actually produced! The West signal box was at the crossing at the end of the north platform; in later years this cabin was an incongruous Midland version brough here from Chevet near Wakefield,when that block post on the MR main line became redundant on 19th. August 1933. East of the station was a small goods yard on the south side, plus an unconnected gas works, leading to a long headshunt,while opposite was a long refuge siding which was available for both directions through slip points. As the layout here was on a curve and with a minor level crossing involved, East box was provided on the north side, beyond which the line ran off to the south east.

Habitation at Snaith was confined to the south of the line, as marsh was on the other side down to the river. Hard by the line was the old Grammar School of early date alongside the priory church of St. Lawrence with its beefy tower looking as if some giant had hammered it well and truly into the ground. South of this was Snaith Hall, complete with a small conservatory which is probably a Paxton structure. Nothing is quite as grand, however, as Cowick Hall which reveals its smart French style facade between the villages of East and West Cowick to the south as our line resumes its straight and level course eastwards towards Rawcliffe. First crossed is Snaith Road crossing which takes in the main A614 trunk route from Doncaster to the coast, after the motorway. This was fairly unusual in that it had a low bridge incorporated on the east side of the highway which light and low vehicles could use when the gates were closed. Next came Mill Lane crossing before the station was reached at 23 m. with yet another level crossing by the earlier road at West Gate, where was to be found the signal box on the south side. This was latterly a structure of LMS design, believed to date from March 1939. At the east end of the platforms was a further level crossing worked by a gate box, this the more important village street along which the place lay, running north towards a large green and junction with the main road to Boothferry. To the south this road ran to Rawcliffe Bridge and an industrial area by the canal. The station building at Rawcliffe, a solid red brick affair which is still available to view at present, especially if one is not too distracted by the passing parade on the nearby M62 motorway, is north of the line at the east end, originally along with a small yard of three roads and a coal staith. The configuration of the roadways caused the outlet of the yard to face westwards, presenting some difficulty for eastbound trains manipulating pick-up traffic.

Rawcliffe yard sported a 5 ton crane, as did Snaith and, not unexpectedly, Knottingley where there was also a small 1 ton 10 cwt. crane at the Depot. Monkhill had to make do with a crane of three tons, as did Featherstone, while the remaining stations managed as best they could wihtout any crane power at all.

West of Goole

The line continued to run south east for just over a further mile to the settlement of Rawcliffe Bridge, where a bridge is to be found over the Aire & Calder canal and Dutch river which run parallel at this point and from where all three headed north east for the port of Goole. On the curve were established a large paper mill, a tar and resin works and a slab works, presumably concrete, not toffee. None was rail linked before 1906, but Turner's paper mill had gained a siding on the south side after 1910 when Rawcliffe Bridge Jc. was opened, providing a new double line to Goole station on the NER. Actually the L & Y line ran into the new Selby-Goole line at Oakhill Jc.,1152 yd. away, the new access opening when all passenger traffic was diverted over it, from 1st. May 1912.

56 087 passes Whitley Bridge Jc. (to Eggborough) with 6K86 empties from Drax to Selby in June 1987.   *S. Batty*

Lord Beverley's Siding was, prior to the construction of the new line, on the south side of the old line by the Old Drain which led to Decoy farm, a very wild place. When the new line was opened, the siding was shifted to it, at Oakhill Jc. and given a decent length with a slip and a trailing connection to the down line. This was actually more convenient for his Lordship, being nearer to his property, though what he did with his facility is not clear, unless it were to do with livestock movements and feed supplies, as was usually the case. The information was somewhat hard to come by, but it appears that the Earl of Beverley was one of the titles bestowed upon George Percy, incumbent of Percy Lodge to the north of the line. A tangible reminder is the elegant clock tower erected by public subscription on the part of the villagers of Airmyn nearby to commemorate his assuming the title of Duke of Northumberland in 1865.

On the Selby-Goole branch a new station was opened, Airmyn & Rawcliffe, midway between the two villages, the former being some two miles away, however, and about twice that distance from Rawcliffe.

To return now to the original line. From Rawcliffe Bridge Jc. the run was due north east alongside the river and canal. Where the original Lord Beverley's siding had been,a new signal box sprang up, Beverley Sidings on the south side at 1157 yd. from Rawcliffe Bridge, with 35 levers and centrally positioned to control the outlet of sidings on the north side eastwards, followed by Beverley New sidings, also on the north side where was to be found an up goods line, this actually on the wrong side of the layout, which became next an up,then a down siding as it ran east, ending up as a down through siding as it neared the next block post at Engine Shed Jc. On the south side of the line the Canal sidings came in by the signal box, five lines squeezed in by the water and running into the up running line.

At 1161 yd. came Engine Shed Jc., also on the south side which, together with the locomotive depot, sidings and junction formed an impressive picture to passengers in a NE section train passing across by the overbridge. Here the five long sidings resolved themselves into three behind the box, only to become five again once a reception line was taken in off the up main and the spur of double line had left to climb up to the NER Dutch River signal box at 470yd. It must be remembered that up to 1911 all L & Y traffic for Hull went this way until the opening of the Oakhill Jc. line, which offered an easier gradient and approach. From Beverley Sidings on the north side the accompanying extra line became down sidings Nos 1 & 2, singling past the turntable, then turning out again as Coal lines 1 & 2 alongside the shed, taking up the shed roads into an outlet opposite the signal box. The frame had 40 levers, latterly an NE replacement with seven spares. The loco. shed had six dead-end roads with a spare line outside and three coal stacking lines. The shed and associated lines here closed on 27th. October 1969, one month before Beverley Sidings box, though Engine Shed Jc. soldiered on until 20th. May 1980.

The shed was on a bleak site and the Author remembers visiting it one snowy day with a keen wind blowing. One supposes that with all the land owned in Goole by the L & Y the shed site could have been chosen nearer to the docks, if only to consider train crews who must have braved atrociously early hours in the mornings and often inclement weather when signing on. The path lay from Marriner's street in Goole along the dock goods line and beneath the NER bridge for a total of $1\frac{1}{4}$ miles. It was left to the enthusiast to savour the atmosphere of the location.

Along the rising spur to the junction at Potter's Grange at 1560 yd. (the old cottage here was 'Potter') with the NER there were first four up sidings at the foot of the gradient and three long down sidings rising with the spur to join it part of the way up at Dutch River signal box which was built to face the NE embankment and lay between the two lines, at the point where the L & Y maintenance became NER. Its strategic importance was doubtful, as it seemed only to control the exit of a long up siding on the NE line which stopped just short of connecting with the L & Y system in the docks-a sort of broad hint, perhaps ? Latterly there was more in the way of sidings here.

In the docks

The L & Y line passed beneath the NER route as double track but soon fanned out again once it was clear, with the running lines skirting the edge of what was basically two blocks of sidings, those to the north presenting ten neatly ranged buffer stops as the down yard, while alongside came thirteen dead end roads in echelon and eight through lines comprising the down yard plus an extra pair of up and down lines alongside the originals, all reaching a tidy junction at Goole Goods signal box on the down side with the original up and down main line running behind it. From Goods Jc. a double line went north east to pass between the municipal water tower and the NER line, becoming four tracks to curve eastwards and there south round Railway Dock, serving it and Aldam and Ship Docks. In view of its closeness, one might almost add St. John's church also! The other line from Goods Jc. passed straight into four terminal sidings at the side of Lower Bridge street after dividing into four further lines which went on to cross the latter street and reach the Railway Dock, and four other lines which ran to various sheds and warehouses at the Ship Dock.

The original main line ran on independently to a coal drop at the side of Railway Dock.

The four terminal lines mentioned above would also have crossed Bridge street to run to the passenger terminus with its frontage on Aire street just south of St. John's. The northbound exit to Railway Dock cut off the lines in due course, while the construction of Aldam Dock made short work of the terminus buildings.

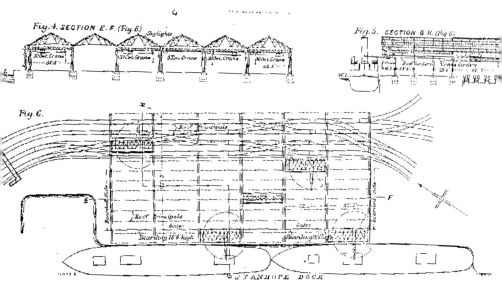

The Lancashire and Yorkshire railway shed at Goole docks

To attempt to summarise developments at Goole Docks: Originally the Aire & Knottingley canal reached the site past a small boatyard to the north, followed by a basin on the opposite side before the Bonding Dock was reached between the canal and Albert street. Passing beneath Bridge street the canal entered the Barge Dock, at the end of which, to the left, the Ship Dock could be entered, this running south-north. At the north end of this, one could turn west to enter Railway Dock, also north-south or east to the Steamship Dock, from which the main lock led into the Ouse, adjacent to a dry dock. It was also possible to gain the Ouse directly from the Barge Dock through an irregularly shaped harbour and a further lock.

The station was along the north side of Railway Dock, with two platforms each of 220 ft. and two centre lines, the area under cover for one half of its length and situated immediately south of St. John's street. As the line ran in there was a two road engine shed on the north side. In due course the Aldam Dock was built to the north of the Ship Dock; it was opened in 1881 on the site of the old Market place. The Stanhope Dock was added as an extension to the Railway Dock in 1891. In many respects the original plan was left untouched and simply added to, with South Dock coming in 1910, West Dock following in 1912 west of Railway Dock.

With the opening of the NER route from Thorne to Staddlethorpe Jc. in 1869 and of the spur from Engine Shed Jc. to Goole passenger, from September 1870 the L & Y was able to develop its traffic to Hull with a new express service to and from Liverpool and gained one member on the board of the Hull Dock Company. In due course an L & Y goods station was opened in Hull in 1886, while running powers were exercised from Goole and an engine shedded at the Hull depot which became No.12

on the L & Y list. Once the new Aldam Dock had been planned, the old passenger terminus disappeared and from 1st, 0ctober 1879 all services used the NER station via the spur.

As coal was one of the major commodities moved around the docks, two wooden coal tipplers were built besides the Stanhope and Railway Docks by Ormerod, Grierson & Co. in 1879, later to be replaced by metal structures. A new goods yard was laid out in 1884 and in 1914 Clegg Bros were awarded the contract for a large yard of exchange sidings to the west, for up to 2,250 wagons.

It is easy to forget that the actual dock system at Goole belonged to the Aire & Calder Canal Co. and that the railway provided the facilities to load and unload merchandise. An interesting instance was the Ghent and Antwerp shed at the side of Stanhope Dock which was hard to work with but one single crane fixed centrally and reaching only any single truck placed on the nearest line. On the waterside there were no cranes, and ships' own derricks had to be employed to transport heavier materials. These would be deposited on the dockside, so that manpower would be wastefully employed in barrowing them to whereever needed. The L & Y Chief Engineer, D C Rattray and CME G Hughes decided to improve matters and, in 1917 produced a goods shed of similar length and width to the old, but with four cranes, each movable, two covering the four available tracks and two the dockside. One crane was 3 tons, the rest 30 cwt. There were originally seven bays facing the dockside; these were reduced to six larger ones which matched the position of the hatchways on a typical L & Y continental steamer. The cranes, being beneath the roofing, had underslung, horizontal jibs and ran on appropriate trackways. Manual handling was largely eliminated and a saving of up to 30% in loading and unloading was brought about.

There were, around the docks, five appliances for discharging wagons into ships' holds and five for lifting up the canal tubs, or 'Tom Puddings' for the same purpose. The 'lift' involved here could well be up to 50 tons. The L & Y also used a 25 ton crane for fuelling steamers, as well as a 30 ton and 20 ton hydraulic hoist.

And what of Goole itself? Britain's most inland port seems to be doing nicely, with ships always visible in dock and a steady procession of lorries arriving and departing along the motorway. The dockland skyline is still intriguing with its distinctive towers and, of course, the church. Of the town itself less can be said, being largely unmemorable apart from the clock tower, a busy main street with various shops and, at the end, a smart library with art gallery and museum opened in 1968 by C.Day Lewis. Much is told here of the town's history. There is also the obligatory leisure centre, which is well equipped with pool and all necessary facilities towards the restoration of a sound body. In Aire street is the Lowther

Ex L & Y 'Pug' tank No. 11207 out near the NER line at Goole

C.T. Goode

hotel, Goole's oldest building which was completed for the opening of the port. Here is a banqueting suite, in which murals show early scenes of activities in the docks.

Until recently some tickets bore the name 'Goole Town', to distinguish the present station from the old one in the docks when it was still in use. The NER station is still unchanged in general detail from its original form, with a good approach from the town side to a long, single storeyed building of standard pattern for the period. The Hull platform has a long waiting room and both sides are well canopied in their original state. The town side at the north end had the goods yard and warehouse, while on the Hull side, north end, were a set of sidings for coach standage, shared with the L& YR. For an NER station the provision of signalling was relatively modest, and in the thirties a form of semi-automatic signalling evolved round the swing bridge just to the north and left the level crossing signal box at Boothferry road in charge. The footbridge has disappeared, leaving only the pedestrian subway beneath the crossing.

Today the station is unstaffed for much of the day and is left to the tender mercies of local amorous layabouts, leaving one to surmise as to how long it will survive.

Methley to Pontefract

The L & Y branch from Pontefract Monkhill to Methley Jc. was mentioned in some detail and related to other companies' lines in the Author's work on 'Castleford'; in fact there is a useful plan of the lines at Methley on p.19 of that work, This system of railways was a proper tangle, and the L & Y contrived to cut a straight course due south east from Methley Jc. on the MR main line and leave Castleford to its left. First met with was Methley Jc. L & Y station; there was a Methley station beyond the junction on the MR-a simple affair on a curve with the signal box on the south side opposite to the goods yard of two roads. A minor road linked this site to the other station nearby of Methley South on the Joint line from Lofthouse. The latter was more pretentious as regards its building and ambitions; here was a small junction with four platforms on the curves, with the left hand fork running downhill to join the L & Y route at Lofthouse Jc. signal box on the north side, just prior to the crossing of the Aire. The right hand fork went off to join a spur, also from Methley Jc. MR to the NER line nearby. Both the Methleys existed here because of each other, to compete over the small amount of traffic which must have been generated. The L & Y had the edge with its goods yard, while the Joint station made do with three odd sidings fitted in off the running lines in convenient places. Lofthouse Jc. was 788 yd. from Methley Jc. L & Y, while that station lay just 248 yd. from the starting point on the Midland. Some 1050 yd further on the line crossed the NER line to Normanton and the junction with the aforementioned Joint line, arriving at Whitwood Sidings cabin on the north side which controlled the entrance to a set of nine sidings which swept off south into Whitwood colliery made, as one might expect, much more of a fuss over by the attendant NER who managed an extra running line at this point.

From Whitwood Sidings to Castleford station, later called Cutsyke to avoid confusion, was a run of 1171 yd. to a place where a rudimentary station existed, of two parallel platforms adjacent to Featherstone road, with no proper signal box, no goods yard and crude buildings. Its location was well out of town to the south and would be unknown to many of the residents who would use the more opulent and centrally placed NE establishment. Beyond it, Cutsyke Jc. at 444 yd. was on the south side and the point where a spur came round from the NE station, one which was to become important in the running of NER services to Pontefract, among other advantages, none of which helped traffic on the direct L & Y route to Methley Jc. The A 639 road crossed here on the level. Beyond a siding was put in on the north side for goods and livestock traffic, after which the line ran on to Glasshoughton at 937 yd. on the south side. Cutsyke Jc. was destroyed by fire in 1974 and replaced on the opposite side by a new cabin.

Above: Prince of Wales Colliery signal box.   *Pontefract Libraries*

Below: Remains of Methley L & Y station in 1958.   P. Cookson

Above: Last day of Baghill-Leeds service, at Monkhill in November 1964
R. Rockett

Below: Collection of buildings that was Castleford Cutsyke station.
J.R. Nowell

From now on for the next mile or two was the section of line which the L & Y could regard as almost its own exclusively for revenue earning, as it served the collieries at Glasshoughton and Prince of Wales, both to the north. Whitwood, an old colliery begun in 1840, was shared with the NER, but these others were more or less reliant on the L & Y, though Glasshoughton did send some coal out towards Castleford along a private tramway. The mine opened in 1869 and up to 1912 there was a triangle to run out coal in both directions, and eight reception roads. In 1912 coke ovens were opened next to the colliery with attendant connections to the main line, a move which brought into use a second cabin here, Glasshoughton East at 614 yd. This layout was bounded on the east side by Carr Gates level crossing before the race course appeared.

The A 639 road passes beneath the line on a skew and neatly separated the course on its right from the colliery on its left, with the railway to the north of that. Prince of Wales colliery was founded, again, in 1869 by John Rhodes, along with a brickworks here. Rhodes was nine times Mayor of Pontefract and negotiated leases from the Trustees of Pontefract Park and Duchy of Lancaster for the working of coal and related minerals.

The colliery and yard are contained on the south side of the line with access at each end, that at the east end closed off by a minor road to Prince of Wales terrace. The colliery signal box, at 1575 yd. was also at this end on the north side. Beyond the road underbridge the line curves round, collecting a loop and sidings to reach Monkhill West cabin at 409 yd. The length of the branch was a little over five miles, beginning with a sharp fall to level over the river, the a rise at 1 in 170 to a summit and a short fall, after which it was rising all the way past the collieries to Pontefract, with a short, sharp 1 in 150 up to the junction, after which there was the relief of a long, similar downhill run to Knottingley. Coal trains hereabouts were quite vocal at times!

The Askern branch

Last but by no means least was the branch line from Knottingley to Askern, actually a part of the through railway system to the North, since it joined the East Coast main line at Shaftholme Jc. and played host on many occasions to such delightful workings as the 'Harrogate Sunday Pullman'. Its length was a little under eleven miles, and apart from a rise of just under one mile at 1 in 720 out of Knottingley, the line fell, first at 1 in 220 to Womersley, then proceeding by gentle grades to its junction. The atmosphere of the line was distinctly rural, apart from the later effect of the arrival of the colliery at Askern in 1911, for which no doubt the curve was put in at Knottingley to bring coal round into the direction of Goole for export. A separate Act was passed for this spur on 15th. August 1915, and it opened to goods traffic on 29th. March 1915. South Jc., where the line joined in, was on the west side of the line, and this box was 555 yd. from Knottingley depot West and 330 yd. from 'B' box at the station.

Norton station in 1960. The building is now the 'Picture Shop'. P. Cookson

From here the line ran fairly straight south east and was furnished with a goodly complement of block posts in the best L & Y tradition. At 507 yd. and 491 yd. came Waterfield Lane Nos.1 & 2 level crossings, before Cridling Stubbs North signal box was reached at 1 m. 382 yd. Both this cabin and its partner, South were on the east side of the line and were 690 yd. apart with an extra down through siding linking the two. From this other sidings went off to a quarry, followed by an extension of the through siding itself to an older quarry at the south end. On the opposite side were sidings for another quarry, alao Rhodes' malthouse (belonging to the coal owner?), these reaching the running lines at the South box. A road crossing ran across three lines at North box, while beyond South box at 521 yd. was the skew Spring Lodge level crossing of the road to Kirk Smeaton. Cridling Stubbs village lay quite close to the railway on the east side, and it is somewhat surprising that no station was built here, with the result that an attractive addition to 'Bradshaw' was lost.

The L & Y was not averse to name-dropping, as witnessed by the reference to Lord Beverley on the main line. At 344 yd. came Lord Hawke's Siding, also on the east side, of 23 levers and named after Earl Stanhope, the landowner and incumbent of nearby Womersley Hall. Here

51

were two parallel sidings on the west side with access from either end and a run into the Northfield quarry. A little further away was Stapleton Park, a grand affair owned prior to the coming of the line by Edward Robert Petre, the estate proving a pleasant rustic backdrop.

After a run of 1 m. 294 yd. the first of the three stations on the branch, Womersley, was reached. Here was a pretty little station which remained untouched for the whole of its existence, with parallel platforms and a small goods yard on the west side, and level crossing at the south end with signal box beyond on the east side. The station building was one of the attractive Swiss cottage types, on the west side and well within the exertions of the villagers close by. The Hall, also, was but a short walk away. Roughly $1\frac{1}{2}$ miles south of Womersley the line was crossed by the H & B main line, the same as mentioned at Heck above, opened in 1885 and here without any resulting spurs or connections. To the west was the H & B station of Kirk Smeaton, set in a lovely spot in one of the best locations for miles around. On closure of the meagre passenger service in 1931, the stationmaster and his wife had to walk the distance to the L & Y line to catch a train to do their shopping.

An ubiquitous WD passes Cridling Stubbs North box in 1957. P. Cookson

The next station, Norton, was 2 m. 950 yd. distant and was, in effect, the identical layout to Womersley in yard, platforms, station building and signal box location, except that the level crossing was more of a skew type. The yard, also, had a larger headshunt but the Swiss cottage was the same. The signal box was similar to others on the branch, having a hipped roof and designed by the Gloucester Wagon Co., though no wheels were provided on these models! Norton village was strung out along the road in the same fashion to the west, while to the east on the common were Bradley's springs in a shallow quarry, obviously an undeveloped natural, medicinal resource.

On the sinking of Askern colliery, opened in 1911, a double line was put in to service the yard which lay to the west of Askern village and whose outlet had, perforce, to run due north for a considerable distance to reach the main line which it could only do conveniently at Norton. Thus it ran in as a single connection on the west side just south of the existing layout and level crossing, with crossover and a convenient water tower on the opposite side. Most traffic would obviously head northwards, but it was possible to run round trains which were destined for Doncaster and beyond, either on the approach line or by fouling the main line and crossing for some time. The colliery yard was a model of lateral neatness, with five reception sidings and ten sidings at the pithead itself though the village tended to cower in the shadow of a growing slag heap.

Askern station, with train at the far platform.   *Colln: C.T. Goode*

Askern station was reached after Selby Road crossing was passed at 1299 yd., a busy one with the A19 and a short way to the south. Askern was right in the village, with a small yard and a goods depot with the luxury of a five ton crane on the west side, then parallel platforms, level crossing and signal box on the west side beyond it. The station building was not ornate this time, as there were no gentry to encourage, though Owston and Campsall Halls were quite close. Instead there was a sturdy red brick structure of the Rawcliffe pattern at the head of the approach on the west side.

Pre-colliery Askern had nursed aspirations as a spa town, as opposite the station was a small lake surrounded by the Manor, Terrace, Charity, South Parade and Cold Baths, the largest building being the first mentioned. A footpath ran round the water, linking up all these delights, though the sulphur well lay at some distance across the field. There were three hotels, while the small hydro lay to the west of the main road.

When the colliery came, only the Charity and Terrace sulphur baths survived, while the Hydro became the miners' welfare Institute, rather in the manner of occupation by a foreign army. The South Parade bath became a rug works, no doubt to employ the female labour, while a cinema now occupied land adjacent to the graveyard. Most interesting perhaps was the new housing estate of 26 terrace houses in groups of four neatly laid out at Instoneville opposite the new Askern hotel and recreation ground. Further development was to come west of the colliery and east of the town level crossing in due course.

From here the line continued until it reached Shaftholme Jc. on the GN main line, with Arksey station, formerly Stocksbridge $4^3/_4$ miles from Askern and a further two miles te Doncaster. The GN did of course have an interest in the stations on the Askern branch; the station at Knottingley was jointly owned.

New notes on Knottingley

The completion of new staff accommodation at Knottingley on 18th. January 1993 led to modest celebrations and the production of an interesting booklet by BR's area Manager, giving some details about 'Knottla' as it is known locally. The town was set on a limestone bed next to the Aire and this became a centre for burnt lime used in agriculture and roadstone. There were at one time 15 quarries in the area; now only two remain. With the arrival of the canal the stone was distributed quite easily and boat yards were set up, making sea-going craft as well as barges. Of these, one yard still survives. (Harker' s) .

Above: No. 90081 comes round the curve from Knottingley to Monkhill near the new curve in 1966. *P. Cookson*

Streethouse West signal box *M.A. King*

As mentioned, the station at Knottingley had five platforms, the sixth line being for stabling and known as the York road. The old engine shed could house four or five engines of the 0-6-0 and 2-4-2T types. This closed on 1st. July 1922, upon which most men were transferred to Wakefield and Goole.

In 1966 the station and old yard buildings went, while a new shed was built in the triangular layout to the east of the station, for which a large mound of limestone had to be lowered to gain a level site. During construction work the remains of an old wagonway were found here, running from the present Rockware glass works site, beneath the Askern and Goole lines, then by a cutting lined with elms, through a tunnel and down to staithes on the canal.

It was planned in the 1880s to build locomotive and carriage works east of Knottingley, probably where the Depot was; however, nothing came of this and the idea was moved to Horwich, the land here being used for setting up creosote vats to 'pickle' sleepers. Today the site holds Knottingley High school and one hopes that the vats have gone! The new diesel depot at Knottingley opened in 1966 with two Class 47s and 27 staff, one engine working to Ferrybridge power station, the other to Thorpe Marsh power station from Frickley and South Kirkby collieries alternately. Very soon the depot came into its own with major workings to Eggborough and Drax powers stations when these came into action. There were also trips to York with coal from Kellingley and Prince of Wales collieries for use in north east power stations.

In the 1970s Knottingley depot, with 13 Class 47s succeeded in moving 440,000 tons of coal in one single week.

The power stations

Of the three powers stations served by the railway under review, that at Ferrybridge 'C' is the odd one out, being administered by Powergen. The earlier station on the site was 'B', opened in 1957 on 20 acres and with a chimney of 425 ft. which was tall for its day. Production stopped in 1977 and demolition of the cooling towers followed ten years later. The new 'C' station had eight 375 ft. cooling towers and it is worth mentioning the great gale of 1st. November 1965 which blew three of them down during construction. There are two chimneys of 650 ft. in height and, one more relevant statistic, the amount of coal burned per hour on full output is 800 tons, which empties a lot of coal wagons!

National Power manages the other two, Drax being commenced on its site in 1965 and generation begun in 1974. At Eggborough construction began in 1962, with generation beginning in 1967.

No. 56 104 at Sudforth Lane, Kellingley in September 1981   *S. Batty*

Passenger services

During the nineteenth century the passenger services were remarkably well ordered and generally consistent, based heavily on Knottingley as a place in which to change trains to and from the various spokes of the railway wheel. The timetable included all the relevant services on one sheet, even with the Wakefield-Barnsley service for a time which needlessly tended to complicate matters. In November 1858 services ran between Leeds Central, Wakefield Westgate and Kirkgate and Knottingley, with four only running through to Goole and three return. Three ran express to Doncaster via Askern(e) after Knottingley and four ran back, the star being the Leeds-Doncaster which left Knottingley at 10.30pm Sundays included, and the return daily working which left Doncaster at 12.35am; these would be mail trains. Stoppers on the Askern(e) branch were two each way, not however arranged on any out and home basis.

On Sundays there were two trains to Goole and return, and three to Doncaster and back.

In October 1864 things had improved somewhat with ten trains between Wakefield and Knottingley, most from Leeds Central five through to Goole and eight on the Askern (no longer with the extra 'e') branch. Four of these were expresses, two started at Kirkgate and one went as far as Askern only. It appears that one or two of these workings also began at Knottingley. The return workings were similar, with at least two stoppers

General view of Knottingley, from 'B' box, with BR 'Standard' locomotive leaving on empty stock. 　　　　　　　　　　　　　　　　　*P. Cookson*

missing out Norton en route. The train which finished its run at Askern does not feature as a return from there, either, which presupposes an empty stock working. On Sundays in 1864 there were two trains to Goole and one back, but three each way on the Askern branch. The mail, which is included, still left Knottingley at 10.00pm but was Up only.

By September 1873 various refinements had appeared, with the addition of Tanshelf and the spur at Goole linking the L & Y line to the NER station there. This meant that at this time trains could be run to both stations in that town. As well as the service for Leeds Cen. through Wakefield Westgate, there was now a service from Leeds Wellington over the Midland and the Methley branch giving a service at Castleford and adding to the fun at Knottingley. This did not, however, operate on Sundays.

At Knottingley there were now seven trains from the Leeds Cen. direction and nine in the reverse direction, give or take the odd working which started or finished at Wakefield Kirkgate. There were now seven trains to Goole, of which two ran into the old station and the rest to the NER with Hull connections. The Askern branch was now more restrained, with six stopping trains up and eight down, each taking generally half an hour. From Goole there were nine departures, three of which ran from the old station, including one express between Goole and Knottingley, probably a train from Hull which had left there at 10.00am, then Goole at 10.50 and arriving Knottingley at 11.21am.

On Sundays there were three trains to Doncaster from Leeds Cen., another which began at Kirkgate and two to Goole L&Y station. The return trips were similar. Six trains each way called at the new station at Castleford on the Methley branch between Leeds and Knottingley, on which there was no Sunday service.

July 1887 saw the introduction of the H & B element into the merrygoround of services at Knottingley, where staff must have had a whale of a time sorting passengers and their luggage into the correct carriages. Now the Goole line was more important, with nine trains from Kirkgate and ten back again, as the Westgate influence had now disappeared. Most trains had a Hull connection either at Knottingley over the H & B to Cannon Street, sometimes with a change at Carlton, or at Goole, where the L & Y terminus had now closed, to Paragon. There was a service of six trains each way between Leeds MR and Knottingley, while the Askern branch saw seven each way, all stopping to Doncaster. The Barnsley timetable was now printed separately to avoid confusion. On Sundays there were an early and a late working to Goole and back, and with no Sunday service by the NER to and from Hull, the 3.00pm from Cannon St. was shown as connecting into the 5.13 to Wakefield at Knottingley. Off the 8.08pm in the other direction passengers could catch the H & B service due in Hull at 9.50. One gem was a brace of Sundays only trains, as follows:

Doncaster dep:	3.05pm	Askern dep:	6.30pm
Arksey dep:	3.09	Arksey dep:	6.38
Askern arr:	3.15	Doncaster arr:	6.45

This was probably a GN working. A station master's hat will be awarded to any reader who can offer a good reason for this one! There was also an additional Saturday only service from Kirkgate to Pontefract Monkhill at 9.00pm.

Matters were more sophisticated by January 1891, with a few extra Saturday workings and the start of those rather irritating conditional footnotes which were more confusing than useful. There were nine down workings to Goole and ten up, all stopping trains,while on the Askern branch eight trains ran to Doncaster and nine returned, still taking half an hour for the run with stops. One service, the 1.20pm from Knottingley, reached Doncaster at 1.45 and was rather mysterious; probably a working from York. It carried a lengthy footnote:

Whitley bridge station elevation to railway

60   *Whitley bridge station elevation to road*

'Stops at Womersley to take up for Doncaster and south thereof. Stops at Norton to set down from NE stations and take up for Doncaater and south thereof. Stops at Askern to set down from York or to take up for south of Newark.'

This must bear some sort of record for its length. Such restrictions have recently found their way back into BR timetables; one morning service at least on the Nottingham-Grantham line has a 'stops to take up only' condition at Bingham, a condition which must be difficult to apply nowadays.

Back to 1891, and the Leeds-Knottingley service was six trains each way on weekdays only, with a late evening Tuesday and Saturday working to Leeds. On Sundays there were two workings each way to Goole and to Doncaster and back, these timed to connect at Knottingley. (See p 64). The earlier Sunday jaunt from Doncaster to Askern was now over, but run on a Saturday instead when it was perhaps more in demand:

Doncaster dep:	3.00pm	Askern dep:	3.25
Arksey dep:	3.05	Arksey dep:	3.33
Askern arr:	3.12	Doncaster arr:	3 40

The point of this run is still unclear. On Saturdays, too, a working left Featherstone for Kirkgate at 3.35pm and Goole for Snaith only at 9.45pm, while an extra working left Pontefract Monkhill for Kirkgate at 9.50pm.
By 1914, as in the case of many things before the first World War, the timetable had reached a peak, with some thirteen trains each way between Wakefield and Goole, of which two were express en route between Liverpool/Manchester and Hull:

Manchester dep:	9.05am	Liverpool dep:	2.10pm
Hull arr:	12.43pm	Hull arr:	5.13pm
Hull dep:	9.05am	Hull dep:	6.40pm
Liverpool arr:	12.20pm	Manchester arr:	9.18pm

The run between Kirkgate and Goole was covered in about 37 minutes. Hours were becoming more ambitious now, with a 4.50am Sharlston-Kirkgate and a similar short working at 5.15pm, probably for miners' requirements. There were also short runs to Sharlston at 5.25am and 1.35pm S0. On Wednesdays a working left Goole at 10.30pm for Snaith only, following market day, extended to Wakefield on Saturdays, while at 10.55pm S0 a late train ran from Wakefield to Goole, arriving at 12.11am. On the Askern branch there were seven trains each way and an extra one doing the late round trip on Saturdays, as follows:

Knottingley dep:	9.30pm	Doncaster dep:	10.50pm
Doncaster arr:	10.03	Knottingley arr:	11.17

The Leeds Midland-Knottingley service remained at six workings each way; the connections at the latter place all remained efficient. The Sunday service was once more the regular one of one morning and one early evening working each way on the Goole and Askern branches. The H & B Knottingley service had been taken off during the miners' strike of 1912 and never restored, as it was found that the costs of running and of renting Knottingley station exceeded the income received.

Grouping had just taken place, bringing the smaller companies into the Big Four, and the LMS was now in charge of affairs. In 1925 there were twelve trains each way on the Goole line, including the two expresses which left Liverpool at 9.02am and 2.00pm and Hull at 9.12am and 6.45pm. There were two short working each day between Knottingley and Sharlston, while the short working at 10.30pm from Goole to Snaith had moved from Wednesday to Saturday only. The 7.15am from Goole to Wakefield now went through to Bradford Exchange. One interesting item was that the 9.25pm SX from Wakefield to Knottingley waited 20 minutes at Featherstone-probably someone's assignation at the railway hotel nearby! On the Askern branch there were seven trains each way, but none on Sundays, the Leeds-Knottingley service now being nine trains each way. On Sundays there were only two trains each way between Wakefield and Goole, but there was now a connection joining the 4.45pm to Goole which left Hull at 6.50am-just imagine waiting over eight hours for a connection on this day of the week at this location. The other train which reached Goole at 8.02pm fared better, as the connection reached Hull at 9.10pm. The link was the unique four wheel petrol ex NER railbus which was based at Selby and ran light to Doncaster on Sundays to work between there and Staddlethorpe where it connected with the Leeds-Hull trains.

In the years before the 1939 conflict services generally reached a peak once more with eleven trains each way on the Goole line, the expresses included, eight on the Askern branch and the same number on the Leeds line from Knottingley. From here, too, there were the early and mid-afternoon trips to Sharlaton and back, and the 9.00am from Goole went on to Bradford. A late service from Doncaster at 10.50pm went on to Wakefield on Saturdays only, while a newcomer to the charts was a daily arrival at Knottingley from Blackpool Cen. during the summer months. On Sundays the morning and early evening services ran as follows:

Goole dep:	7.57am	4.45pm
Wakefield arrs:	9.13	5.59
Wakefield deps:	11.10	6.45
Goole arrs:	12.15pm	7.45

At Goole all but the first had a connection to or from Hull, and what is interesting is that a railcar or a push and pull unit was involved out and home from Goole. This would point either to a loan by the LNER or an LMS unit of some kind being out-stationed.

Wartime brought restrictions and reduced services on the Goole line to seven or eight trains each way, with six or seven on the Leeds run. There were no extras in the way of short workings or Saturday runs. The Askern branch had a morning working leaving there at 7.23am and reaching Leeds at 8.42, the commuters or war workers, as they were known at the time, leaving again at 5.35pm and back in Askern at 6.37pm. This odd service persisted until final withdrawal in 1948. What must have contributed to the truncation was the difficulty of slotting the LMS trains into paths on a busy main line to Doncaster which would cause time to be lost for both parties.

As things settled down again after the war so the numher of trains on the Goole line increased again, with roughly eight each way, including two each way between Leeds and Goole and one to Goole from Mirfield at 12.28pm SX and Sowerby Bridge at 11.45am SO.; a train left Goole at 4.30pm for Bradford, arriving at 6.00pm. Not to be forgotten were the expresses, now from Kirkgate at 11.48am and reaching Hull at 1.02pm with a stop at Snaith at 12.18 SO, returning from Hull at 6.35pm and reaching Wakefield at 7.46pm. 0ne curio in the 1954 timetable was related to the 10.35pm from Kirkgate to Goole which had a footnote stating that, on Saturday 25th. September 1954 only, the train would start back at Bradford at 9.45pm. One hopes that the train crew had the diary handy! When the NE region took over the running of the line nothing changed for a time and the 1956 timetable is a virtual copy of the one above. For a time, however, from as early as 1880 the NER had run a service of trains from Leeds via Garforth, Kippax, Castleford and up to Pontefract Monkhill, ending up round the spur into Baghill. In 1914 four trains ran this way and three survived up to 1949. From 1958 to 1962 the service was revived using the new diesel units and taking the more direct routes from either Leeds or Bradford, some of the trains also running to and from Hull. Defects in the track formation are said to have been the cause of the closure of the Baghill adventure-'experience' might have been a better word for souls braving the high and curving viaduct approaching the terminus.

Methley L & Y had gone in 1943. When the Wakefield-Pontefract Monkhill line closed to passenger traffic, a diesel service between Leeds and Knottingley was instituted from January 1967, serving Cutsyke, as Castleford L & Y had now become and with some trains extended to Goole. However,the Methley Jc.-Cutsyke Jc. section closed in 1968, along with Cutsyke station, and now all services used the spur from Methley Jc. to the NER station at Castleford, reversing here to run round the second, southerly spur to Cutsyke Jc. and along to Pontefract. Prior to this upheaval, in 1966 there were ten services each way on the Wakefield-Goole line, with seven outward starting from Westgate and two returning there (shades of a century earlier). The through run was at least ten minutes quicker. On the Leeds-Knottingley line there were three workings each way, all calling at Cutsyke. Embedded in the timetable were still to be found the old expresses which had survived for many years:

Kirkgate:	11.47am	Hull dep:	18.30
Goole:	12.34pm	Goole dep:	19.03
Hull arr:	13.02	Wakefield arr:	19.45

Both now called at Monkhlll and Knottingley ,the first also honouring Snaith by halting.

In due course the lines mentioned were duly absorbed into the West Yorkshire Metro-train pattern, with the old Barnsley timetable appearing as part of the whole, much as originally. Thus, the hourly Leeds-Sheffield service via Barnsley now runs via Methley to Castleford, where it reverses, shunning Altofts & Whitwood to run to Normanton; there is also an hourly Leeds-Knottingley service which, again, reverses and runs via Monkhill station. The 12.07pm is extended to Goole, returning at 13.52, while the17.22 runs to Goole, leaving to return at 18.52. For commuters a train leaves Goole at 7.10am, reaching Leeds at 8.20. The line is single as far as Hensall and, though the rails are still visible under the weeds, there is no sign of usage into the dockland at Goole. Recently a service was re-introduced between Knottingley and Wakefield, reinvigorating the stops at Tanshelf and Streethouse. The line here is double, though the industrial scenery is devastated.

Knottingley as an Exchange station in 1891.

Up.

Wakefield Kirkgate	dep:	7.30am	9.20	10.50		1.40pm	3.20	6.50	7.50
Knottingley	arr:	7.58	9.48	11.18		2.06	3.48	7.14	8.18
Leeds Well.St.	dep:	9.17		10.50		1.10	3.05	6.35	7.40
Knottingley	arr:	9.52		11.21		1.45	3.40	7.10	8.21
Knottingley	dep:	8.03	9.54	11.25		2.08	3.51	7.15	8.32
Goole	arr:	8.37	10.27	12.00pm		2.38	4.25	7.48	9.07
Knottingley	dep:	8.05	9.55	11.37		2.10	3.53	7.17	8.43
Doncaster	arr:	8.37	10.27	12.10pm		2.43	4.25	7.48	9.15
Hull Cannon St.	arr:	9.40	11.30	1.10pm		3.45	5.25	8.52	10.28

Down

Hull Cannon St.	dep:	6 30am		10.00		12.00pm	1.45		5.15	7.01
Doncaster	dep:	7.23	9.07	10.48		1.20		4.27	6.00	8.00
Knottingley	arr:	7.55	9.33	11.18		1.50		4.57	6.30	8.30
Goole	dep:	7.23	8.57	11.00	12.10	1.15	2.55	4.37	5.58	8.00
Knottingley	arr:	7.55	9.32	11.35	12.45	1.50	3.30	5.12	6.33	8.35
Knottingley	dep:	8.00	9.34	11.41		1.55			5.15	6.35
Leeds	arr:	8.37	10.10	12.18		2.32			5.52	7.12
Knottingley	dep:	7.56	9.38	11.37	12.48	1.58	3.34	5.19	6.38	8.39
Wakefield	arr:	8.25	10.10	12.08	1.20	2.30	4.05	5.50	7.08	9.11

There was also a train from Goole to Wakefield at 6.17am, without any connections.

Through L & Y workings to Hull over the H & B began after 1918. Initially goods traffic was exchanged at Hensall Jc., then two Class B goods trains were run, one leaving Healey Mills at 9.00am and arriving at Springbank West at 1.33pm. The return trip was at 2.50pm, arriving back in Wakefield at 6.05pm. The motive power was usually an L & Y 0-6-0.

Goods working and shed allocations

Freight train working over most lines tended to be difficult to pin down, chiefly due to the number of 'as required services' timetabled, extras put on and, if observations were being made, confusion due to trains running out of course due to delays. In 1950 the following workings were on offer along the Askern branch running north:

Just the ticket. All water taken from the crane must be paid for (at Wakefield).   *M.A. King*   65

Train No.				
500	Empty	Doncaster Mineral to York Holgate	5.20am	
2	Mineral	Bentley Colly. to Gascoigne Wood	7.43	MO
10	Empty	Doncaster mineral to Norton	8.00	
532	Mineral	Bentley Colly. to Gascoigne Wood	9.16	
4	LMR Mineral	Bentley Colly. to Crofton Hall	9.40	MX
6	Class B	Bentley Colly. to Gascoigne Wood	9.40	MO
4	LMR Mineral	Bentley Colly. to Crofton Hall	9.50	MO
540	Class B	Decoy Yard to York	10.16	
8	LMR Mineral	Bentley Colly. to Knottingley	1.33pm	
30	Exp. pass	Skegness to York	1.46	SO
570	Empty	Doncaster Mineral to Nrth Stockton	2.12	
590	Empty	Doncaster Mineral to York	4.50	
614	Class B	Decoy to York.	8.55	

Up

1	Mineral	Gascoigne Wood to Bentley Colly.	6.20am	
5	LMR Empty	Goole-Bentley Colly.	7.30	
7	Mineral	Gascoigne Wood - Bentley Colly.	8.10	
9	Mineral	Norton - Doncaster Mineral Yd.	10.45	
3	LMR Empty	Healey Mills - Bentley Colly.	11.05	
527	Mineral	Fryston Colly - Decoy.	7.17pm	

Train times for the above are passing Shaftholme Jc.

The following also passed Shafthome Jc. as stated in the summer of 1984

Up

04.20	6L74	Middleton Towers - Monk Bretton.	
08.40	6L58	Lindsey Oil Refinery - Ferrybridge or Drax power stations.	
			MTTh
19.58	6L50	Middleton Towers - Knottingley.	SX
21.35	795	Belmont Down Yard - Folly Lane ICI.	

Down

02.19	6E26	Folly Lane - Belmont Up Yard	MX
09.34	6H39	Monk Bretton - Middleton Towers.	MSX
13.54	6D39	Ferrybridge or Drax - Lindsey Oil Refinery.	MTThO
19.08	6F83	Tees New Yard - Parkeston.	SX
22.10	6P38	Knottingley - Middleton Towers.	SX

The following trains passed Hensall during the same period:

05.06	6D67	Dringhouses - Hull.	MSX
06.09	6D67	Dringhouses - Hull	MO
09.06	6L58	Lindsey Oil Refinery - Drax	MTThO
- - - -	7L24	Healey Mills - Kellingley (arr. 16.20)	WFO

Wakefield loco. depot in 1970.   *M.A. King*

Shed Allocations at various locations (courtesy, L & Y Society.)

Wakefield Shed (Code No.6) 1908.

4-4-0 Aspinall 6ft. 923,926.
4-4-0 Aspinall 7ftO3in. 1096,1099,1101,1106,1111.
4-4-2 Aspinall/Hoy. 711,1394,1400,1412,1413,1414.
0-6-2 B-Wr 5ft.1in.188,276,6030
2-4-2T Aspinall. 98,119,192,369,514,525,721,1014,1047,1173,1259,1264,
1331,1344.
0-6-2T B-Wr 4ft .6in. 145.
0-6-0ST B-Wr/Asp. 238,284,292,533,549,556, 560,593,647,749,761,783,
800,845,859.
0-6-0 B-Wr/Asp 933H.
0-6-0 Asp 'A' Class. 4,33,338,326,343,422,437,462,466,648H,650,652,
684,1024,1025,1059,1080, 1083,1091,1121,1122H,1133,1134,1135H,
1140H,1141,1187,1236,1292,1299,1300.
0-6-0 Asp/Hughes 255H.
Hughes/Schmidt S'htr. 898H.
0-8-0 .Asp.190,378,395,822 1431.
0-8-0 Hoy Circ. F'box. 396,434,1436,1438.
0-8-0 Asp/Hughes. 1453,1454 1458,1459,1481,1483,1484,1485,1487,
(B-Wr = Barton-Wright)

1490,1475,1477,1480.
0-8-0 Hughs Comp. 1475 1477,1480.

Plus two other shunting tanks and 37 goods/coal engines. Total: 147.

Knottingley Shed.(Code No. 9) 1908.

0-6-2T B-Wr 5ft.1in. 276 (out-stationed Wfd.) 0-6-0 Asp.A Class. 82,213,290,450H.Total: 5.

Goole shed. (Code No.10). 1908

0-6-2T B-Wr. 5ft.1in. 252,691.
2-4-2T Asp. 90,1034,1268,1271.
0-6-2T B-Wr.4ft.6in. 146.
0-6-0ST Asp. 166,545,547.
0-4-0ST Asp. 155,377,403, 729,814.
0-6-0 B-Wr/Asp. 934,942,943,950H,954,955,956H,957,959,960H,962, 967,968,969H,974,976.
0-6-0 Asp A Class. 135,152H,1077.
0-6-0 Asp/Hughes. 829h
0-8-0 Asp. 1427.
0-8-0 Hoy Circ F'Box 1439.
0-8-0 A3p/Hughes 117,1488.
Plus five other passenger tanks and 11 other goods/coal engines. Total: 59.

Wakefield Shed 1921.

4-4-0 7ft.3in. 1096,1099,1101,1106,1111.
2-4-2T 1044, 1014,1047,1173,1259,1264,1331,1344,98,119,192,369,514, 515,525,721.
4-4-2 1394,1400,1412/3/4,711.
0-6-0ST 238,284,292,533,549,556,560,593,749,761,783,800,845,859.
0-6-0 A. 4,33,212,228,255H,261H,326,343,422,428,437,440,462,466,647, 648H,650,652,684,1024,1025,1059,1080,1083,1091,1121,1122H 1133,1144,1135H,1140H,1141,1187,1236,1292,1299,1300.
0-6-0 Superhtr. 93H,195,234H,483H,818H,898H,1366H.
0-8-0 Saturatd. 83,87,91,95,190,201,378,396,406,412,413,434,463,511, 611,616,617,628,635,656,666,697,709,736,739,792,820,822,831,866, 880,894,906,911,912,914,1365,1430,1440,1453,1454,1458,1475,1477, 1481,1483-5,1487,1490,1492,1493,1496,1497-9,1586,1587,1590,1591.
0-8-0 Superhtr. 6,7,59,150,235,241,281,312, 395,460,493,603,640,915, 1431,1436,1459,1547,1553,1555,1556,1558,1559,1563,1564,1566,1568, 1570,1572,1575,1577,1580,1581,1584,1585,1610,1612,1613,1615,1616, 1618,1627,1629,1634,1635,1636,1637,1640,1644,1645, 1646-8.

Knottingley Shed. 1921.

No allocation. Subshed of Wakefield. Generally post 1919 a Class 27 or 28 0-6-0 outshedded from Tuesday to midnight Sunday/Monday. Crew were lodged in the district.

Goole Shed. 1921.
2-4-2T 90,1034,1268,1271,1541,1542-5.
0-4-0ST 28,32,64,155,377,68 (On loan ex-works)
0-6-0ST 166,545,547.
0-6-0 B-Wr. 934,942,943,950H,954,956H, 957,959,960H,962,967,968, 969H,974,976, 0-6-0 A. 135,152H,1077.
0-6-0 Superhtr.891H,893H.
0-8-0 Saturated. 108,512,612,1427,1488,1588.
0-8-0 Superhtr.117,134,1439,1578,1607,1608,1620,1621,1623.

Wakefield Shed. Spring 1961. Code No.56A

Stanier 2-6-2T 40117,401 55.
Stanier 2-6-4T 42649,42650.
Hughes 'Crab' 2-6-0 42862,42863.
Ivatt 2-6-0 43075.
Johnson 0-6-0 43705.
'Jinty' 0.6-0T 47255,47266,47379,47571,47572,47573.
B1.4-6-0 61015,61017,61024,61131,61268,61296,61385.
Thompson 01 2-8-0 63857,63920.
J50 0-6-0T 68904,68910,68933,68939.
WD 2-8-0 90047/61. 90076.90100/112/116/230/326/341-2. 90339, 90348/353/363/370/379/380. 90385/396/415/417/429/497/498. 90581/604/607/615. 90620/625/631/633/635/639 90651/654/656/ 679/710.
Diesel D2587-93.

There was a record total of 39 WD locomotives at this shed.

Goole Shed. spring 1961. Code No. 50D

Ivatt 4MT 43097-8.43125.
Ivatt 2MT 46407-8.
'Jinty' 0-6-0 47462,47438,47581/9.
Ex L & Y 'Pug' 0-4-0T 51222,51241/4.
WD 2-8-0 90044/94.90186/213/228/260/265/478/531.
No.51222 was at the same shed in 1908 numbered L & Y No.377.

8F No. 48084 slips round the back at Monkhill with a load of coal off the Methley branch.   *R. Rockett*

Information on local collieries.
(Courtesy British Coal and R. Rockett.)

Prince of Wales.   Opened in 1869. First coal cut in 1872. Still working. *

Snydale (Victoria). Opened c.1867 on an older site. Brickyard opened on site of coke ovens in 1934 producing 6 million bricks per annum.

Sharlston Opened in 1861 on an older site. Expanded in 1865. Closed in 1993.

Ackton Hall (Featherstone). Opened in 1888. Closed in 1985. Glasshoughton Opened in 1885. Closed in 1986. Coking plant opened in 1912, closed in 1979.

Kellingley . Opened in 1960s. Still working. Askern. Opened in 1911. Closed in 1991.

Savile. Near Methley. Opened in 1860. Closed in 1985.

*Under threat at time of writing

Boiler Explosion.

(From the item by Driver Derek Thompson in the brochure for the Knottingley Open day in April 1993.)

'On the evening of March 11th. 1901 an L & Y 0-8-0 No.676,known as a coal engine, or Tiny, built in 1900 at Horwich works was travelling tender first from Glasshoughton colliery to Goole with 52 wagons of coal on a downhill grade of 1 in 150 from Knottingley to Sudforth Lane. On the rise to the canal bridge the boiler exploded, fatally injuring the driver and fireman. The boiler came to rest fifty yards away in a field, creating a hollow which formed a pond which remained for many years. Of the 52 wagons, 24 left the rails, with ten going down the bank.

Major Druit and Mr. Carlston, Board of Trade Marine Engineers, concluded that the fault lay with a large number of roofing stays being in a bad state of corrosion and being made from inferior metal. The CME for the L & Y, Mr. A. Hoy, stated that, in his opinion the fusible plug had melted because the locomotive was short of water. The Board of Trade disagreed, as no evidence of crown plate burning could be found, as would have been expected with overheating of the firebox .

Major Druit judged the driver to be free from blame and No. 676 (LMS No. 12706) was reboilered and eventually withdrawn from service in August 1927'

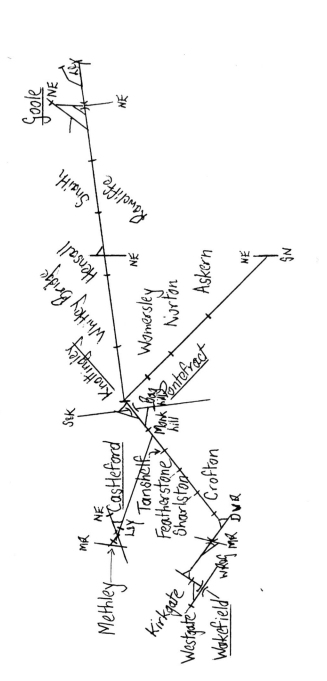

The WP & G and associated lines

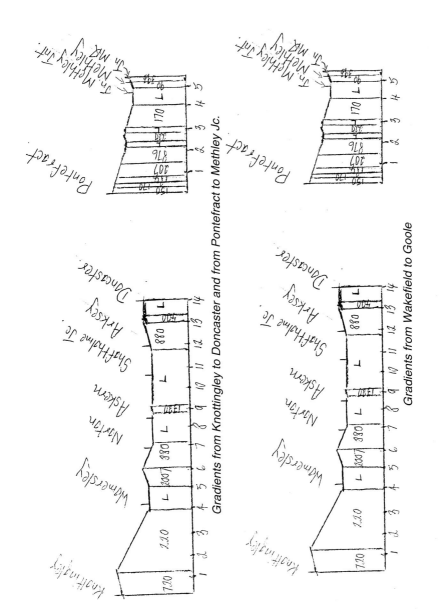

Gradients from Knottingley to Doncaster and from Pontefract to Methley Jc.

Gradients from Wakefield to Goole

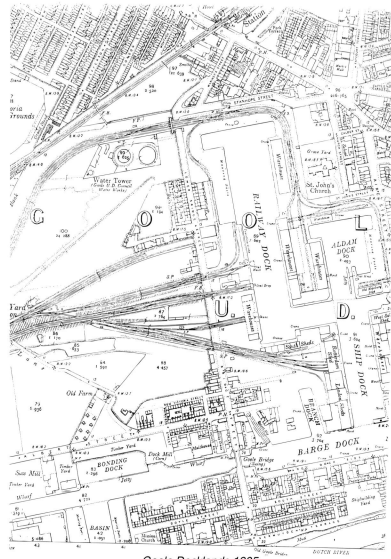

Goole Docklands 1905

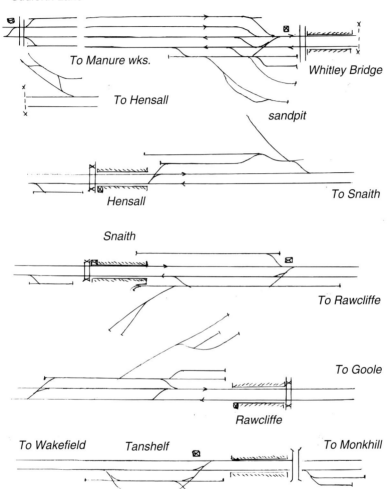

Sudforth Lane

To Manure wks.

To Hensall

Whitley Bridge

sandpit

Hensall

To Snaith

Snaith

To Rawcliffe

To Goole

Rawcliffe

To Wakefield   Tanshelf   To Monkhill

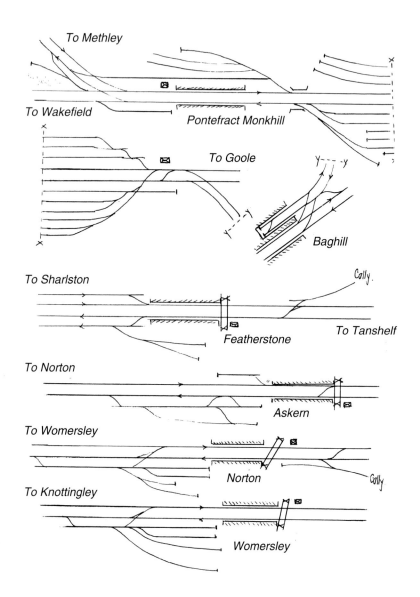

To Methley

To Wakefield

Pontefract Monkhill

To Goole

Baghill

To Sharlston

Cally.

Featherstone

To Tanshelf

To Norton

Askern

To Womersley

Norton

Cally

To Knottingley

Womersley

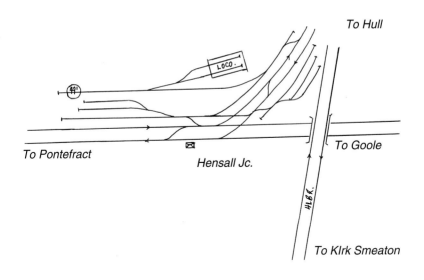

To Hull

LOCO.

To Pontefract

Hensall Jc.

To Goole

To KIrk Smeaton

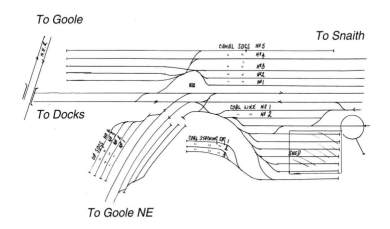

To Goole

To Snaith

CANAL SDGS No5

To Docks

COAL LINE No 1

COAL STACKING SDG 1

SHED

To Goole NE

Engine Shed Jc.

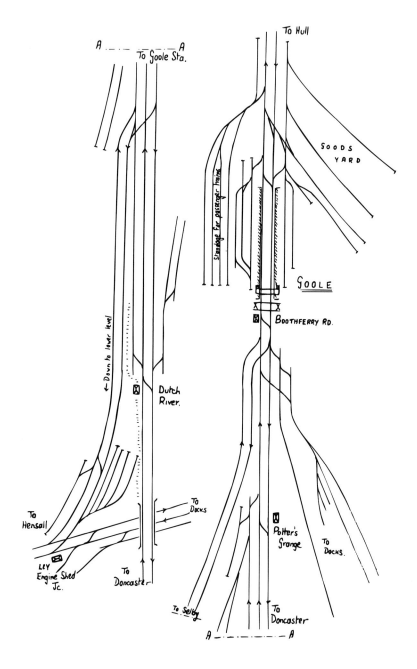

A ----- A
To Goole Sta.

To Hull

GOODS
YARD

Standage for passenger trains

GOOLE

BOOTHFERRY RD.

← Down to lower level

Dutch
River.

To
Hensall

To
Docks

LⁱY
Engine Shed
Jc.

To
Doncaster

To Selby

Potter's
Grange

To
Docks.

To
Doncaster

A ----- A

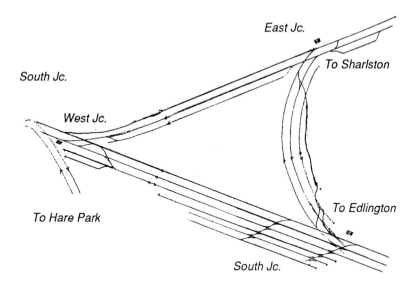

Junctions at Crofton

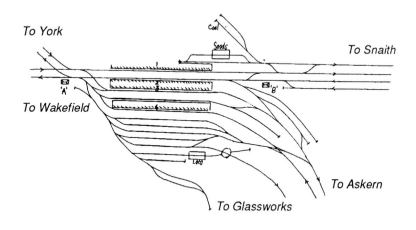

Knottingley

Books by the same Author uniform with this volume:

The Dearne Valley Railway.'
'Huddersfield Branch Lines.'
'The Railways of Castleford.'
'The Selby & Goole Railway' (Oakwood Press.)
'Railways in East Yorkshire' (Oakwood Press.)

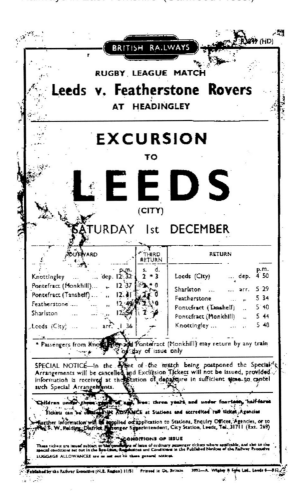